The
Judas Kiss:

Growing Beyond Betrayal

The
Judas Kiss:

Growing Beyond Betrayal

John Brownlee

Clovercroft Publishing

The Judas Kiss: Growing Beyond Betrayal

© 2021 by John Brownlee

Published by Clovercroft Publishing, Franklin, Tennessee

Published in association with Larry Carpenter of
Christian Book Services, LLC
www.christianbookservices.com

Edited by Ann Tatlock and Sara Huron

Cover and Interior Layout Design by Thatcher Design

Printed in the United States of America

978-1-954437-24-1

Dedication

To my mother, sisters and grandmother who, like me, had to battle back from a major betrayal.

And to all my readers who have overcome the betrayal they did not expect.

Acknowledgements

Nothing one does in this life is totally independent of others. Therefore, I am very grateful to many who have assisted me immensely over the years in dealing with betrayal and helping me think through the concept of betrayal and prepare *The Judas Kiss* for publication. While many have helped in many ways over many years, I want to give special recognition to the reviewer's whose comments are listed in the Foreword, and my friend Jay Thatcher for the cover design and my daughter Mary for her artistic consultation.

Most of all I thank my Heavenly Father who has given me grace and strength to make this journey through the challenges of life and betrayal.

Foreword

Betrayal is an unhappy and sometimes traumatic event, experienced by the majority of the population. Some have successfully overcome it and others are still on the overcoming journey. And others are stuck in the anger stage. Even for those who have overcome it, it often leaves a deep scar on the psyche, resulting in the individual becoming a better or bitter person.

The Foreword of most books is written by one major supporter of the author. We have chosen to have many readers from many walks of life in US and Canada who have reviewed the manuscript share their comments. You will likely find at least one reviewer you can relate to.

John Brownlee has dedicated his life and career to understanding and supporting those who have experienced emotional and interpersonal suffering and challenges in primary relationships.

His work regarding betrayal, *The Judas Kiss*, is a thoughtful attempt to comprehend how betrayal occurs and its lasting effects. Beyond the impact of betrayal, John's intent is to provide the reader with support and guidance toward understanding and meaningful recovery.

RANDALL W. PHILLIPS, PhD, LMFT
AAMFT CLINICAL FELLOW
MEMPHIS TN

The Judas Kiss by John Brownlee is a comprehensive analysis of betrayal. It provides numerous real-life examples of betrayal to which we can all relate, including painful personal examples of betrayal from his own life. *The Judas Kiss* also details how best to respond when betrayed and gives specific coping recommendations that will benefit all of us. I highly recommend this book.

DAVE SANDERSON
RETIRED INTERNATIONAL MARKETING EXECUTIVE
ONTARIO CANADA

John's book was especially helpful to me for giving me the insight and tools to confront my deep-seated anger and hurt. It was especially helpful to understand my betrayer is not unique; his character is like other con men. John nailed so many personality characteristics, I gasped while reading. John truly understands. I know now I will never get closure with my betrayer as he does not feel remorseful; only honest individuals do. John's Points to Ponder helped me explore my true feelings and awareness. Thanks to this book, I am on the road to forgiveness.

LORI WHITBEY
CONTENT MARKETER
NASHVILLE, TN

My favorite chapter is Chapter 12 because John Brownlee has identified and described betrayal trauma, and has encouraged people to not blame themselves. Because my area of specialty IS this topic, it is one of the most difficult traumas (and really the core issue with most trauma) to heal from. There was not a least favorite chapter.

MELISSA BRADLEY BALL, MS

A LIFE COACH SPECIALIZING IN TRAUMA

BIRMINGHAM, AL

As I read through the table of contents, my interest was piqued to read the chapters. My favorite chapter was "Overcoming the Pain" because of the examples and strategies you shared with us - the readers. And this line particularly got my attention: "You did not have control over who deceived you or how you were deceived, rejected, or betrayed. You do have control over how you are going to respond and live." This thought is one I share with my clients on a regular basis. And, I didn't have a "least favorite" chapter. I thought the entire book was well worth the read.

DR. SYLVIA ANN TRAPUZZANO,

LICENSED MARRIAGE & FAMILY THERAPIST

THERAPY IN THE PARK, PALM DESERT, CA

John Brownlee has been a trusted advisor of mine for over 40 years. His counsel has been wise and reliably useful to me both personally and professionally. In his latest book, The Judas Kiss, John provides a practical road map for anyone dealing with betrayal, forgiveness, and seemingly insurmountable past issues. His counsel comes from a place of proven professional qualifications and the hard-won wisdom gained from personal experience. We all have pain that robs us of freedom and joy if we don't work through it correctly. The insights in this book will help the reader journey to a place of forgiveness and freedom. It has enabled me to think clearly about the lingering pain of betrayal in my own life. If you are ready to cast off the chains and heal the scars of betrayal, this book will help you too.

JIM TUNE, PRESIDENT IMPACT MINISTRY GROUP
SENIOR PASTOR EMMAUS CHURCH
ONTARIO, CANADA

He gets it ... John Brownlee truly understands the stabbing pain of betrayal. He has heard it expressed by so many wounded people, and he has experienced betrayal ... himself.

What do we do with the puncture wound it causes? In this book we can see the results of two differing ways of dealing with it. We can leave it open and untreated, but it will likely become more "infected" with anger, guilt, bitterness, etc. Or we can learn from this author how to cleanse and ultimately receive relief from our wound.

I believe that this book will provide the sparks to ignite hope and healing in so many of us who have suffered "The Judas Kiss" of betrayal.

CINDY HOTTINGER
MOTHER, HOMEMAKER, AND LONGTIME FRIEND OF
THE AUTHOR
NASHVILLE, TN

I have known John Brownlee for nearly my entire life and have always found him to be a trustworthy friend and colleague, able to cut through the dross to reveal the truth of whatever situation I present to him. His most recent book, *The Judas Kiss: Growing Beyond Betrayal,* is no different. John brings his years of experience to the topic of betrayal, offering hope to anyone who has been betrayed whether in their family, work, or community life. You'll find good wisdom and common sense on every page.

SARA HURON, CPCC, PCC,
EXECUTIVE AND LEADERSHIP COACH,
ORGANIZATIONAL AND FAMILY BUSINESS
CONSULTANT
CINCINNATI, OH

In his work, *The Judas Kiss,* John Brownlee takes us on a journey through the personal impacts of betrayal. Using examples from his own life and decades of counseling, John shows how betrayal leads to a complexity of emotions that can manifest negatively if not acknowledged and carefully managed for healing to occur. I found his approach to be clear and concise. I will certainly be using these ideas and steps in my practice as a counselor and life coach. His closing words in Chapter 13 resonate strongly in me and are needed by many people I counsel – "It is not your fault!"

DEBBIE BOWYER
MASTER ACCREDITED COUNSELOR AND WHOLE-LIFE
COACH
NOVA SCOTIA, CANADA

Contents

Introduction: Meet Judas 19

Chapter 1 Portrait of a Betrayer. 21

Chapter 2 Character Traits of a Betrayer 37

Chapter 3 Rejection or Betrayal?. 57

Chapter 4 Betrayal in the Family. 69

Chapter 5 Generational Betrayal. 95

Chapter 6 Betrayal by a Friend 103

Chapter 7 Self-Betrayal. 111

Chapter 8 When You Betray Others 131

Chapter 9 Betrayal by the Church. 139

Chapter 10 Betrayal by the Community. 151

Chapter 11 Your Reaction to Betrayal 161

Chapter 12 Overcoming the Pain 169

Chapter 13 Growing Beyond Betrayal 187

Appendix How We Learn to Betray 199

Notes 203

Introduction

Meet Judas

The story of Judas, who was also known as Judas Iscariot, is very interesting. On one hand, his story is well known. On the other, people do not know the full story. They only know that he was a betrayer.

In the first century and prior, the name *Judas* was very common. (In fact, there were two Judases in the chosen twelve, Judas the brother of James and Judas Iscariot.) It was a Greek name meaning "God is thanked." *Iscariot* signified that Judas was "the man from Kerioth," a town in the south of Judea (most likely the present-day Palestinian town of Hebron).

Judas was one of the twelve men chosen by Jesus of Nazareth to be part of his inner circle. He traveled and participated in most of Jesus's ministry. Judas carried the purse to cover the financial needs of Jesus and the twelve disciples. According to the biblical New Testament, Judas stole from that common purse.

Judas is most known for betraying Jesus for a fee of thirty pieces of silver. The Bible describes how, in the dead of night,

Judas and a cohort of Roman soldiers approached Jesus while Jesus was praying in an isolated place. Judas kissed Jesus on the cheek, having prearranged the kiss as a signal to the soldiers that the one he kissed should be the one they arrest.

The Bible also shows that Jesus knew Judas would betray him. Historians still don't know why Jesus would knowingly choose someone to be part of his inner circle whom he knew would ultimately betray him.

I'll share more of Judas's story throughout the book. I have chosen him as the exemplar for this book on betrayal because he manifests the characteristics of the typical betrayer. Throughout this book, you will see attributes of Judas that are similar to the traits of your betrayer—traits similar to those of the one who kissed you on the cheek and then betrayed you.

You are not the only one who has been betrayed, so don't beat yourself up as if it is all your fault. It is *never* your fault. All of us have been betrayed by at least one person, probably even more. What is more important than whether you've been betrayed or by whom you've been betrayed is how you deal with and get beyond it without letting your betrayer do serious long-term damage.

May this little book about Judas and my experiences help you understand your own. May it help move you beyond your betrayal, to a more healthy and fulfilled life.

Chapter 1

Portrait of a Betrayer

Judas's kiss of betrayal has reverberated across the past two thousand years like no other. It has permeated every country and every culture regardless of that society's religious beliefs. Simply mentioning the name *Judas* evokes the thought of betrayal in most people. For some, it evokes not just the concept of betrayal, but the memory of being betrayed. Some of us have been betrayed more than once.

Why has this particular betrayal had more impact than any other in history? Was it because Judas betrayed a man who was recognized by many as the Son of God? Even those who do not acknowledge Jesus as the Son of God still see him as a good man or a prophet who did not deserve to be betrayed and then die a horrific death by crucifixion. Was it because the betrayal was initiated with a kiss, an honored sign of affection?

This betrayal by the man named Judas is so repugnant that no one in the world names their child Judas. The name has become synonymous with betrayal. Have you ever heard of anyone naming their newborn son Judas?

Others have initiated very destructive acts that had a great impact on history. Names of these scoundrels, such as John Wilkes Booth or Lee Harvey Oswald, are instantly associated with an evil deed of betraying or killing a great man. They were assassins and cowards. They committed their act then hid from the public. They betrayed not just one person, but their entire country. Some betrayers destroy their victim physically and others destroy one's reputation or their emotional psyche.

Still, Judas's betrayal is the one that represents them all. His closeness with Jesus, his membership in Jesus's inner circle, the political nature of his act, his secrecy, his suicide. He represents them all.

What Is Betrayal?

Betrayal doesn't happen when someone takes aim at, or takes down, someone they think of as an enemy. No, betrayal hits closer to home than that. Betrayal is the breaking of trust in a once-fond relationship. The betrayer usually has a direct relationship with the one or ones they are betraying.

Victims of betrayal never deserve to be betrayed. No victim is a perfect person—who is?—but no person deserves to be deceived or spoken of in an evil manner behind his or her back.

Victims of betrayal tend to blame themselves for not seeing it coming. Stop it! We are all prone to deny the presence of dangerous people in our lives. Betrayal is not your fault.

In the Revolutionary War, the traitor/betrayer Benedict Arnold was first a war hero in the American army. He then switched sides and sold out to the British for money. Interestingly, when my children were attending public school in Canada, they came home telling me about Benedict Arnold being a hero. Being the American I am, we had quite a discussion of whether Arnold was a hero or a traitor. While one may debate if Benedict Arnold was a patriot or a betrayer, there is no doubt who Judas was. Usually there is no doubt or gray area when someone betrays.

For over three years Jesus had treated Judas as a friend and even trusted him to be the treasurer for his twelve hand-picked followers. With all that trust and responsibility, why then did Judas betray his friend, the one who had treated him so kindly? Some have suggested that he sold out for thirty pieces of silver—the equivalent of about five weeks' wages. Today the value would be about six hundred dollars.

Judas was probably not completely motivated by the money. Possibly his real motivation was that Jesus would never be what Judas wanted him to be. Maybe, Judas wanted Jesus to use his power to overthrow the Roman army and give him a place of authority in the new regime. (Certainly not the first person who betrayed to get political power.)

There is a common theme with Judas and most betrayers. Betrayers are always angry at someone because they cannot get from them what they want and for some reason they want to elevate themselves. Often the victim does not even know their betrayer is unhappy with them. The fact is they are usually angry at themselves and blame others.

Betrayers are always cowards. Judas went in the dark of night to a remote place. He did not have the courage to plant his kiss publicly. Those who betray you are also cowards. They do not have the courage to face you and share their grievances. They always work behind your back, in the shadows of your life. (We will outline the traits of a betrayer in Chapter 2.)

Betrayal starts behind your back, but sooner or later you will learn about it. Rarely does the betrayer announce they have betrayed you or are actively betraying you. You stay in relationship with this person, someone you consider to be your friend. Which is why betrayal is such a dishonest, destructive act. You expect trust, loyalty, faithfulness, and confidentiality. Instead, you get treachery, deception, faithlessness, and lack of discretion.

The longer the betrayal goes on without you finding out about it, the greater the shock factor when you learn the truth. (The greater the shock factor, the more likely you have been betrayed.) And then your first reaction is denial with expressions like, "I really don't believe this." You may even be angry at the messenger.

Rarely does the full scope of the betrayal come out all at once. The betrayer when confessing will vow they are telling the full and complete story. As a therapist, I have heard the *"This is the full truth. I am telling you everything"* spiel too many times. While I suspect there is more happening than is being told. Our human nature is to tell as little as possible. We all learned that trick in childhood. The less we tell, the lighter the punishment. You can probably still hear your parents say, "Come on now. Get it all out and let's get this over with." I bet you a hundred dollars you never spilled all the beans. I know I did not, and I still harbor secrets from the past.

We have all been on the nasty end of being betrayed. Just when we think we have learned every fact, another piece of information comes to our attention. We will hear more bits of the betrayal over a period of weeks, months, or even years. Some are minor details and others shockers. Each time we hear another piece it jabs into an old wound.

For example, betrayers are very good at devious behavior. Their actions may not be seen immediately, but in time they do come to light. For example, my father was a betrayer. He betrayed our family in many ways, but we did not know all his betrayals for many years. It was many years before we knew he cheated my sisters and me out of an inheritance. And he sold our family's cemetery plots to pay his bar tab. And much, much more.

How well you dealt with the first wound will determine how hurtful the new revelation is. Hopefully you have dealt with it in a healthy way so you can say, "Oh well, I am not surprised," and quickly move on. The degree that you are able to do this will indicate how well you really have dealt with it.

Life—since the beginning of time—is full of betrayal. Artists—historians, poets, and musicians—use their means of expression to convey the pain of betrayal. William Shakespeare, an astute observer of life, frequently detailed stories of betrayal. In *Richard III*, Richard betrays his friends and family and in return his friends and family betray him. Betrayal is so common that throughout the play the audience is not surprised or shocked with any intrigue, even when Richard orders the execution of his nephews whom he had committed to protect. In *King Lear*, the lust for power knows no bounds. Edmund even betrays his own brother. And the Ides of March (March 15th) has become popularized due to the betrayal and assassination of Julius Caesar.

In biblical literature we see eleven brothers sell their younger brother into slavery. And Jacob, coached by his mother, deceives his father to get his father's blessing.

In the political realm, intrigue, betrayal, and corruption are constant. Episodes are so common that we do not even need to give illustrations.

Betrayal is about character. It is not just what one does; **it is who one is.**

Betrayal has everything to do with the character and behavior of the betrayer and little to do with the behavior of the victim. Yes, the victim is crushed but usually betrayal is not the result of their behavior. If you are the one betrayed, the only part of the betrayal that is about you is how you handle it. You did not choose to be betrayed; you only get to decide if this horrible situation will be a stone that crushes you or a building block that you step on to move forward to new awareness and maturity in your life.

Betrayal is about deceit. Deceit is the distortion of the truth for the purpose of misleading someone. It is about *consciously and intentionally* manipulating with the intent to present a false image of oneself or a situation. Typically, deceit is not an instantaneous or one-time act.

It is very important to note that I say *typically* because sometimes someone makes a one-time slip. When that happens, the action is not a large part of who they are. You must discern whether the behavior is out of character for this person. At first you will probably think it is out of character, but as you look at it more closely and over time you will likely see the pattern.

Once confronted, does your betrayer attempt to cover up or blame others? Or are they genuinely remorseful? Do they readily admit their mistake, apologize, and attempt to make amends? If so, then it is likely a one-time action. If, however, you continue to study their behavior and you identify a pattern, it is more likely a character issue. Now you are dealing with another thing altogether.

The primary focus of this book is twofold: to help you identify a betrayer and to help you get through the hurt and move ahead in your life.

Trust Is at the Core

At its core, betrayal is about breaking trust. Before betrayal there had to have been trust, and with trust, some degree of relationship. Perhaps there was even love. The relationship was probably not at the same level for both parties, though the victim assumed it was. The greater the trust and the deeper the relationship, the greater the hurt for the one who is betrayed.

Trust is one of—if not the most important—trait essential to all productive and healthy relationships. Marriage, families, friendship, faith, the economy, and democracy are all built on the foundation and expectation of trust.

Without trust, a relationship is in constant turmoil and conflict. In chaos. We can barely live a minute without trusting someone. We must trust every time we eat something, drive or fly someplace, accept the word of our employer that we will get paid, put our money in the bank, or plug in an electrical appliance. The list is endless. Our lives totally revolve around trust.

We are always navigating the conflict between trust and mistrust. If we have been betrayed or deceived more than once, our tendency is to move toward mistrust. Getting hurt by someone we've trusted is extremely painful and we are inclined to avoid as much pain as possible. However, the dilemma is that mistrusting everyone is also very painful. We find ourselves alone and insular, and we can even become quite paranoid. All paranoia is built on the fear of being hurt again. Each time we have been betrayed, deceived, or cheated on it becomes harder to trust.

If we are going to live a growing, productive, happy life, we must choose to move beyond the pain. With my clients, I have often compared emotional pain to an impacted wisdom tooth. You choose either to live with constant pain and take an abundance of pain killers, or to go through the pain of getting it pulled. Howard E. Butt, Jr., in his book *Who Can You Trust? Overcoming Betrayal and Fear*, says, "So, the trust versus mistrust battle rages around and within us."[1]

Trust is very fragile, like a precious vase, and once it is broken it is very difficult if not impossible to mend. And the cracks will always show. I recall counseling a couple where the husband had been unfaithful. He apologized and asked for forgiveness. His wife said, "I forgive you, but I do not know if I will ever fully trust you." Like Humpty Dumpty who had all the king's horses and all the king's men, this couple could not put their marriage together again.

There is a ratio of sorts. The closer the relationship and the more one trusted and lost, and the more chaos the deception created in one's life, the deeper and greater the hurt and the harder it is to recover. Thus, it becomes harder to believe and trust anyone. (More on this in Chapter 12, "Overcoming the Pain.")

And once this pattern is established, the more likely we are to fall into the same trap and betray others.

Betrayal is usually a very calculated act. The betrayer presents the same lies over and over to convince the other person they are telling the truth. Some synonyms of betrayal are *deceit, cunning, dishonesty, double-dealing, fakery,* and *fraud.* Deceit grows like a nasty cancer until the betrayer is so wrapped up in the deceit and lying that they are convinced that what they are saying and doing is justified. The betrayer not only deceives the other person; they also deceive themselves. Often, they come to a point where they no longer know the difference between truth and deception. They come to believe that what they are saying and doing is acceptable, appropriate, and they can get away with it.

This is usually the result of a long process, often starting in early childhood, of lying and cheating to get what they want because they lack self-confidence to step forward and say directly, openly, and honestly what they want and like, or what they do not want and do not like.

At the extreme, deceit and betrayal are pathological—significant deviations from what is considered appropriate human behavior in our society. The victim is shocked because the behavior is outside expected norms. And the victim comes to learn that the betrayal they experienced was likely not a one-time event or behavior. The betrayer's deceitful behavior is representative of their lifestyle, but the betrayer's family and friends just do not want to admit this to themselves. The seeds were planted long ago, just waiting for the right circumstances to sprout.

When we study the character of Judas, we should not be surprised that he was a betrayer. He was ambitious, had a selfish agenda, and was even a thief. He stole from the purse he was assigned to carry; the money he took was intended to provide for Jesus, the disciples, and the poor.

Why Study Betrayal?

Early in my life, I personally experienced the Judas Kiss, which has caused me to devote considerable attention to observing betrayers as a therapist and as a member of society. My first experience of betrayal happened when I was eight or nine years old. Some evenings around nine o'clock my father would come downstairs all cleaned up and wearing a suit and tie. He'd give my mother a little peck on the cheek and say he was going to the tavern. He'd then come home drunk in the wee hours of the morning. Even at my young age, I sensed there was something seriously wrong. Then he started talking about his health and the need to move from our home in northeast Ohio to Florida. Soon the announcement came that he was leaving in a couple of weeks. He would go to Miami, find a job, and then we would move down to join him. As he was about to go out the door to go to Florida from our home in Ohio, he gave each of us a little kiss on the cheek.

Before long, the truth came out. He had planned to go to Miami alright, but instead of taking us—his family—he intended to take his secret girlfriend. He deserted three children and his girlfriend deserted four. He was like most betrayers—manipulative and deceitful—because he did not have the courage to address the situation face on. I had just experienced my first Judas Kiss. The first of many.

Throughout my life and career as a therapist, I have seen it many times, just as some of you have. We know the pain and chaos betrayal can bring.

Yet we should never be surprised by betrayal. (I recall reading the statement, "The worst thing about being surprised is that you are surprised.") So the big challenge becomes: How can I be prepared for deceit, rejection, and betrayal without becoming cynical and paranoid?

Rejection Not Betrayal

Rejection is quite different from betrayal. While being on the receiving end of rejection can be painful, normally the one doing the rejecting is more honest and the act is usually not as devastating.

For example, rejection happens when a person recognizes that they no longer want to be in a relationship. If the person is a person of character, they will tend to be fairly straightforward and have some level of compassion for the other. We'll discuss the differences more fully in Chapter 3, but a betrayer, as opposed to someone who is simply rejecting a relationship, will build a web of deceit and lies over a period of time, as my father did. They may even take things to the point of trying to convince the other person that the problem in the relationship is entirely the other person's fault.

The Development of Character

"What we call a character trait is the appearance of some specific mode of expression on the part of the individual who is attempting to adjust himself to the world in which he lives. Character is a social concept."[2] In other words, character traits are behaviors we use in order to try and become significant and accepted in our society. Beginning early in life, if we believe that we are valued we will develop constructive ways of relating. On the other hand, if we believe that we are not acceptable, we may begin to develop less acceptable ways of becoming recognized and significant. Though relationally destructive, sometimes people choose these less than healthy ways of relating in order to have some power and control over their lives.

The reality is that these individuals may never be fully aware of who they are and how they impact others. In fact, if they were, most would have a difficult time living with themselves. Occasionally an individual will see that they are seriously struggling to relate to others and adapt to their environment, so they will seek therapy to help them adjust. The tragedy is that once they enter into therapy and begin to get a glimpse of who they really are, they may run after just a few sessions. They may worry that their ability to change is limited and they may be fearful of what they may find and of who they may become if they do change. And they may also fear that they will lose their primary ways of relating, feel powerless, and fail to get what they want. They prefer to get what they want through less than honorable ways rather than not get acceptance and respect at all.

Contrary to the big excuse "I was born this way," character traits are not inherited. "They are to be considered as similar to a pattern for existence which enables every human being to live his life and express his personality in any situation without the necessity of consciously thinking about it."[3]

Because it is so difficult for betrayers to see themselves as they are, it almost appears as though their character is inherited. It is clear that character traits are *not* inherited or in one's DNA. While other family members may show the same or similar traits, these are learned from observing and being in the environment where they are demonstrated.

Betrayers use whatever they can to gain a sense of importance and significance in society. These individuals are often very capable and have acquired a high level of education and professional approval, but it does not mean they accept themselves deep in their core. The degree of intelligence or professional achievement will usually not change how they see themselves.

Remember the big financial scandal that was perpetrated by the now infamous Bernie Madoff? Here was a bright, highly educated individual who ran the biggest Ponzi scheme in the history of the country. The recent news coming out of prison is not that he is remorseful, but that he blames the system for being structured in such a way that it is easy to abuse.

I worked for a few years as a chaplain in a medium-security prison. One day the warden called me to his office. He informed me that I needed to go to the women's area of the prison and tell one of the inmates that her son had just been run over and killed running across an interstate. He was running away from the juvenile detention center. I did so, and then I went across the walkway to tell the same news to her brother, who was also in our institution. Then I called downtown to the chaplain of another jail to have him tell another brother, and then I called the maximum-security prison to have the chaplain tell another brother. I had a meeting in my prison before going to the funeral. I knew seven of the eight siblings. So, one might think this is a classic case of heredity or DNA.

Off we went to the funeral, some in handcuffs, others also with shackles and armed guards. Seven of the eight siblings were wearing prison garb. To my surprise, I knew more than half the friends and visitors at the funeral home; they had previously been occupants of our prison. They greeted me warmly and inquired how their friends still in prison were doing. With the exception of the handcuffs, shackles, and armed guards, this funeral was like any other I had attended. To my knowledge, all of them had been raised in the same part of town. Their behavior was evidence of how they had adapted to their environment.

Now of course you may want to ask, "My betrayer didn't come from a troubled environment. How is it that one who was raised in an apparently good family could turn out to have the traits of a betrayer or other anti-social characteristics, especially when the other kids in the family turned out well?" The only answer anyone can give is that each individual decides early in life how he or she sees life and what they must do to succeed in their environment.

The seeds of positive or negative character traits are planted early in life. Some are buried deep. Over time, with the right circumstances, and sometimes in stressful times, the seeds will have a favorable environment to sprout and bear nasty fruit. How often do we hear or say, "Wow! I have known her for many years, and I would never have guessed she would have behaved like that! I did not know she had it in her!" Time and circumstances will ultimately reveal the real character of a person.

In my counseling office, I have heard many "unbelievable" stories of deceit and betrayal where the seeds of unhealthy character development finally came into full bloom. You too have heard your share of stories about betrayal. You have possibly been on the receiving end of the cruel behavior.

One couple had been married for over twelve years and they came to see me for marital counseling. They were finally expecting their first baby, whom they had both said they wanted and were excited about. They described a "good" marriage. And yet, a few weeks into the pregnancy, the husband announced that he did not want to be a father, nor did he want to be married. He was in a longtime secret relationship.

In another situation, a young couple who had been married for five years came to me for counseling because she had just found out that what her husband had told her from the beginning of their marriage was a lie. He had told her that he was an only child and that his parents were dead. Can you imagine the impact on her when she found out his parents were alive, and that he had siblings? When she met his family, she found them to be very likeable people. At first there was no evident reason for his deception. Then the truth came out; he was so embarrassed by his parents divorce he could not admit it. Over a period of time, we worked on trying to reestablish trust. Although they seemed to move forward in the marriage, I have often wondered if she could ever totally trust him again.

Points to Ponder

1. Have I been betrayed? Has it happened more than once?

2. How am I at trusting?

3. Am I pleased with how I have dealt with a trusted friend's betrayal?

4. Am I still blaming myself for being betrayed?

Chapter 2

Character Traits
of a Betrayer

As a therapist and management consultant, I've seen many deceivers and betrayers. They think they are cunning and unique, but they are not. They are deceiving themselves, for one betrayer behaves much like another. The only variations I've seen among betrayers are in which traits betrayers exhibit the most, the level of intensity with which they display them, and how effective they are at using them.

We can lump all betrayers together with the not very flattering term of *con men*. That is a picture we can readily grasp. We have a very hard time seeing someone we either were or still are in relationship with as a con man or woman. We like to trust, and we do not want to be fooled or lied to, especially by someone we know, to whom we have given our trust.

The following traits are listed in the order of what I see as the most predominant. Each betrayer–con man/person over time has chosen certain traits that work most effectively for them. Each person will most likely use many of these traits at different times and to different degrees.

Narcissistic

People who are narcissists have an extreme level of self-absorption, an exaggerated sense of self-importance, and a constant need for attention and admiration from others.

The word *narcissism* comes from the Greek myth of Narcissus. Narcissus was a handsome young man who rejected the desperate advances of the nymph Echo. As punishment, he was doomed to fall in love with his own reflection in a pool of water. Unable to consummate his love, Narcissus lay gazing at himself into the pool, hour after hour, and finally changed into the flower that now bears his name, the narcissus. In everyday speech, *narcissism* often means egoism, vanity, conceit, or simple selfishness.

People with narcissistic tendencies are adept at turning any conversation into a focus on how great and wonderful they are. They love telling you about their achievements and want you to praise them. Often, they take great pride in how they are dressed and style their hair. Although narcissism is thought of as a male trait, it is common among both males and females. We consistently see highly narcissistic men and women on television.

While it appears that narcissistic people love themselves and have a superior sense of ego, the exact opposite is true. People who are the most proud, arrogant, and boastful do not have superior self-esteem. They actually have low self-esteem and are trying to cover this up by overcompensating. When we see people like this, we often use expressions that are very descriptive like: "I want to cut them down to size," or, "I'd like to let the air out of their balloon," or, "They are too big for their britches."

Since narcissism is actually the artificial face one puts on an unhappy and insecure self, these people become actors on a stage and after some time, they come to believe they are the person they are portraying. French philosopher Francois de la Rochefoucauld said it best: "We are so accustomed to disguise ourselves to others that, in the end, we become disguised to ourselves."

I am well acquainted with one who is a very skilled professional actor. The problem is, over time the acting became so ingrained in his personality that he is now very narcissistic. I doubt he knows who he was or who he really is. He, like many other people who display narcissistic behavior, presents himself as superior to those around him.

Liars

It should come as no surprise that narcissistic betrayers are not good at telling the truth. Because they are protecting their weak ego and deceitful lives, they make commitments they do not intend to keep. Lying is one of the human traits that if one does not quickly stop it, it will become a greater and greater problem until the person lying does not know the difference between truth and fiction. Some actually become pathological liars.

My experience and observation in life is that if people become heavy drinkers or alcoholics, drug addicts, or have other major addictions, one can almost be certain that they will have great trouble telling the truth. If we tie narcissism to alcohol abuse or other addictions to betrayal, we have a very unflattering personality. So, if you are around someone who is addicted, be very careful not to expect them to be or do who or what they say. Be on guard.

Deception—lying—can become so common that betrayers even lie about the little things. Other people see it, but they come to accept the betrayer's "exaggerations" as part of who they are. I recall one woman who was such a liar that for years she had consistently listed a university degree on her resume even though she had not even graduated from high school. Later as we were talking about her career, she finally admitted she had not even graduated from high school. Lying is a true symptom of someone lacking in self-confidence.

Manipulative

Betrayers always tend to be manipulative. Everett Shostrom, in his book *Man the Manipulator*, says, "Manipulators are so much a part of our everyday life that the unskilled observer notices only the very obvious or hurtful. They are like the birds which are all about us in the natural world."[1]

The key to understanding manipulators is to know that *they do not trust you, nor do they trust themselves.* Shostrom says, "Not trusting himself for self-support, man believes his salvation lies in trusting others. Yet not trusting the other person completely, modern man manipulates the other in an effort to support himself in the process. It is as if he rides the coattail of the other person and then attempts to steer him at the same time, or to use a more modern analogy, he is a back seat driver refusing to drive yet driving the other."[2]

That is why manipulators manipulate. Because they lack self-confidence though they always appear to be very confident. They are unable to say openly and honestly what they like and want. And because they are dishonest with themselves and others, they do not believe that you will be honest with them. So, because they are articulate, they dance around and maneuver the conversation to get what they want without being straightforward. The more intelligent the individual, the more skillful they are. When it does not go their way, they blame others.

Manipulators are masterful at later coming back, after they have done as they pleased, and denying what had previously been agreed upon. On more than one occasion I have coached a business leader how to understand and manage the manipulator. Write it down in front of them and give them a copy. And better yet, have them sign it with you.

On one occasion a client company asked me to evaluate an employee whom they saw as very manipulative. On the second visit I was able to get directly to the issue and she broke down crying. I just sat and waited for her to finish crying. When she composed herself, I asked if the emotion was genuine or manipulative. She then started to cry again and finally said she did not know. Of course, I never knew if her response was an honest or manipulative one. And I am not certain even she knew.

Shostrom considers manipulative behavior to be self-defeating. It's self-defeating because the person manipulates to get their needs met, but they learn that it only works temporarily. Once their intended victim is on to their game, the manipulator is left feeling more defeated than before.

Self-Serving

A self-serving person behaves in similar ways to the narcissist. Betrayers really only think of themselves. While at times it looks like they are interested in others, follow their actions through and you will see that whatever they are doing, they are doing for themselves. Judas pretended to be totally committed to Jesus and the other disciples when in fact he was not. His plan was to get what he wanted.

Therapists know that when they hear the words, "I am only doing this for your good," they are dealing with a self-serving individual. It is like the person who frequently says, "Trust me." When you hear either of these phrases, be suspicious and stay alert and be very careful about letting them have influence in your life.

Lack of appreciation

Betrayers are not prone to showing appreciation to others who give to them, help them, or assist them. They just take it as though it is expected and go on their way, leaving the one who gave or assisted them a bit stunned and confused. Watch for this pattern early on and become wary of people who show this trait, even when they are in your immediate family. They are probably already violating a core value their parents and other adults tried to teach them when they were young.

A subset of this is what appears to be a complete lack of interest in your time, space, and welfare. They do what they want to do without considering your needs in time, space, or finances. And I think they are so turned in on themselves they are quite unaware of their self-centeredness. When you confront them on this, they often become indignant. They don't want you to approach the topic. They act as if you are offending them. Or they act completely surprised and all you get is a dull look.

After this happens a few times, you back off and stop bringing up issues that are important to you. Thus, the relationship degenerates even more, and trust continues to shrink, such that before long the level of trust is very low. You are then at risk of becoming their servant to avoid making scenes and to keep them from making you feel bad about yourself.

Articulate

In order to be a successful manipulator, the betrayer is usually very good with words. Otherwise they could not convince others of their lies. It seems to me that many betrayers are extroverts who are accomplished interpersonally. It is interesting to note that many have gravitated to careers in politics, the arts, sales and corporate leadership—careers in which the very traits of being articulate, manipulative, and narcissistic fuel their success.

Some manipulators are passive aggressive and come across as weak, dependent, and indecisive. They control you by their weakness, so you feel sorry for them, and soon you become subservient to them.

Low Affect

Although betrayers appear to be affectionate, the depth of their affection is actually very shallow. It would be an oxymoron to say that one is narcissistic and self-focused while at the same time genuinely caring of others. When observed closely one will notice that betrayers never really genuinely or deeply give themselves to others. They just never have and probably never will have a deep bond or love with anyone. That was my experience with my narcissistic betrayer father. In my relationship with him both as an adolescent and an adult, there was always coldness and lack of intimacy. As a therapist and long observer of people, I have seen this verified many times. Interestingly, they like to talk about all the people they have helped.

Blames and Accuses

Betrayers like to blame others for the situation, regardless of how much they are at fault. I knew a husband who was quite certain his wife was having an inappropriate relationship with another person. Each time he confronted her, she aggressively turned on him and accused him of not trusting her; she found choice words to degrade him.

The fact is that she *was* in a relationship and had been plotting for some time to leave. Not long afterward, she did. But she left only after she had everything lined up to go her way—a new job, secret money in the bank, and lies to all her friends and their mutual friends about her husband. This was masterful, but not as uncommon as one may think. Both men and women demonstrate this behavior. Most, like Judas, plot in advance of the betrayal. Some plan for years. Rarely is their betrayal spontaneous.

Most betrayers are excellent at getting people in their social circles to see real or imaginary faults in the one they are betraying in order to deflect attention from their own behavior. This is one of the oldest dirty tricks in the world.

Sigmund Freud called this *projection*—accusing others of the actions you are doing or assigning your own traits to others. It is where one accuses another of exactly what they are doing. This is extremely popular in politics in order to deflect the attention from themselves.

Be keenly aware of anyone who frequently and passionately protests or speaks out against some behavior or vice. Very likely they are already secretly doing it, or about to.

Blamers are people who dare not look objectively at themselves because when they do so, they will see their own unhappiness. Typically, as you observe them over time you will find them less than happy and more prone to be outspoken about all the ills of others and the world. When you examine the life of Judas the Betrayer, it appears he was quite discontent with his lot in life. This is possibly why he was trying to force Jesus to become the earthly king and show his power; Judas wanted to be part of the new regime. What is absent in the recording of Judas's betrayal is any mention of him blaming anyone for his behavior.

Betrayers also demonstrate their tendency to blame and accuse in another way. Typically, they direct harsh words toward others whom they see as betrayers or potential betrayers. They recognize other betrayers for what they are and call them out. They then protest that they would never be like that.

William Shakespeare, a brilliant student of human behavior, consistently revealed his observations in his many writings. One of his most famous observations— "The lady doth protest too much, methinks" (*Hamlet*)—has come to mean that one can insist so passionately about something not being true that people suspect the opposite of what one is saying.

Lack of Remorse

One of the reasons it is so very difficult to get "closure" with someone who has betrayed you is because they rarely accept responsibility. If they say they do, often it just does not feel like genuine remorse. And some of that is because—believe it or not—most are incapable of it. When one has been betrayed and the betrayer has been exposed, the victim is often shocked by the betrayer's refusal to express remorse. Rarely will the betrayer come out and apologize. Even when he was a child and "forced" by his parents to apologize to his little sister, the best he could do was mumble the words, so he could avoid the consequences.

We must understand that not everyone has a sense of guilt or is capable of remorse. A sense of guilt is not something that we are preprogrammed with at birth. Like all other emotions, guilt is learned early in life. Some children develop a high sense of guilt and others do not.

Typically, the betrayer's victim has a much higher sense of loyalty, trust, and guilt than does the betrayer, and the victim just cannot comprehend how this person they have known—or thought they knew—could be so insensitive and without remorse.

Don't confuse guilt with shame. Guilt is what you feel when you have violated your own principles and values. Shame is your concern for how others will see you. Sometimes what you are seeing from a betrayer is shame, not guilt. The betrayer does not want their family and friends to know what they have done. This contributes to their need to blame the other person. They have the narcissistic trait and do not want to be exposed for who they really are.

A few years ago, a well-known political figure was accused of having been in an inappropriate sexual relationship with a young staffer. When the accusations became public, he held a news conference. He looked directly into the television camera and said, "I did not have sexual relations with that woman." Most of the audience believed him because he did not show any sense of guilt. Several months later he publicly admitted to the relationship. The fact is this man betrayed his wife and the entire country and lied about it on national television. Because we see many examples of this behavior in society, why are you surprised when someone you know denies their behavior and does not apologize? You are surprised because you never thought your friend could do this to you. This is the stuff that happens to other people.

Sometimes betrayers are labeled *sociopaths*, which means they have little or no conscience. Not all sociopaths are violent; in fact, most are not. And they rarely are "a dirty old man in a raincoat." One day I was in a social setting when I met a tall, handsome, articulate, and very well-groomed man. I had heard of him and knew he was a very successful orthodontist.

The gentleman said to me, "I understand you work in the prison and know about sociopaths."

"Yes," I replied.

He went on to tell me that his psychiatrist had diagnosed him was a sociopath. He was the first and only person I have ever met who readily admitted to being a sociopath. However, I suspect he was really testing me to see how I would react and if I would be honest with him. We went on to have an open discussion of about what *sociopathy* meant.

Cheaters

We think of betrayers as cheaters. When we follow the trail of someone who betrays another, we often find multiple affairs and clandestine relationships.

They also try to find many little ways to "beat the system." They see it as a game. However, eventually they move on to cheating on bigger things like taxes or misuse of company funds. While they see this as beating the system, they really are being dishonest with others and breaking the trust placed in them.

One woman I knew first committed the classic marital betrayal and then over time her character traits were exposed when she got into legal trouble with the Internal Revenue Service (IRS) and immigration.

Prideful

For centuries, pride has been considered one of the seven deadly sins. "Pride goes before destruction; a haughty spirit before a fall." Many theologians see pride as the core of all other sins including lust, gluttony, greed, sloth, wrath, and envy. When you do a quick examination of these behaviors, you will easily see how many of them match the traits of a betrayer.

When we follow the life of a betrayer, we will often see progressive emotional and behavioral lifestyle deterioration. It is not uncommon to see several unhealthy behaviors such as excessive drinking and other addictions, lack of caring, increased deception, lying, cheating, and sexual inappropriateness. Once a person starts down this slippery slope of betrayal, it becomes very easy to continue this downward slide in morality. They continue because what they have been doing for years has been getting them what they want. And they lack self-awareness, so they do not even know their situation. Oh yes, sometimes it appears that they have changed, but be careful. Betrayal is like any other negative character trait. They do not do it all the time, but when they do, it can be very destructive.

In life there is no such thing as status quo. We, like the environment, are always either growing and improving or deteriorating.

When the Truth Comes Out

In the previous chapter we went into some detail to start profiling the betrayer. Because the points we made are very important, we are restating and highlighting some of the information:

> *Betrayers are always cowards.*
>
> *Betrayers are very good at devious behavior.*
>
> *Betrayal starts behind your back.*
>
> *The longer the betrayal goes on without you finding out about it, the greater the shock factor.*
>
> *Rarely does the full scope of the betrayal come out all at once.*

Remember, when you have been betrayed, you have been betrayed by someone you considered a friend. You expected trust, loyalty, faithfulness, and confidentiality. And instead you were betrayed. As a result, you are left dangling without a resolution of the relationship. You end up being blamed and you feel as though the betrayal was all your fault. You may feel angry or depressed. I have seen countless spouses who just could not believe that after several years of marriage, their spouse, male or female, could act like they did and go on their merry way into a new life, seemingly not troubled by their behavior at all.

Often the betrayed one just cannot understand why they are hurting so badly from what has just been exposed, especially when the betrayer appears to be unconcerned. Nor can the victim get the betrayer to make an apology. Remember the traits we listed earlier? This is because the victim and the betrayer never really had the close emotional connection the victim thought they had.

Betrayal Results in Death

Most betrayers experience a slow death of character and the soul. Others, like Judas, end up physically dead. Unless a betrayer chooses to make a dramatic change, they become more and more hardened and less and less sensitive to the needs and feelings of others. It is just not possible for humans to have a healthy emotional core while breaking trust, lying, blaming, and doing hurtful things to others. Having these negative traits and repeatedly committing damaging offenses against fellow humans can only lead to the emotional and often physical destruction of the offender. Sometimes the self-destruction is also physical because they try to fill their empty self with alcohol, prescription or street drugs, or other substances. They need these substances to deal with their depression and anxiety. And by now, once the behavior is so ingrained, they have reached a place in their lives where neither they nor their psychologist can connect the symptoms to the cause.

After my father left I only saw him a few times in my adult life. On one occasion, he said to me, "I want you to know I have really cut back on my drinking. I have given up the hard stuff and I am down to twelve beers a day." I was shocked at how proud he was at what he thought was a life change. He had modified his drinking, but he really had not changed who he was or his life. He eventually died of cirrhosis of the liver.

The Betrayer's Co-Conspirators

It's not uncommon for the betrayer to have a few friends around them who will participate in the deceit and cover up. Sometimes it is because their friends are much like they are; other times, their friends have also been deceived. I have a former friend who betrayed me and when I brought it to the attention of a couple of his siblings they were not surprised. They already had known about his tendencies, but never warned me. However, once the betrayal has happened and some time has passed, often most of the friends seem to quietly disappear from the betrayer's life.

Judas originally had the support of the leading priests. Here we have co-conspirators with different agendas. The leading priests wanted Jesus dead and out of the way. It is believed by some that Judas wanted Jesus to display his power and establish his kingdom on earth.

After the betrayal, when Judas went back to the leading priests, they did not want anything to do with him. Interestingly, Judas and the priests deceived and betrayed each other. There never is and cannot be long-term loyalty between persons of poor character. This is commonly displayed in our ubiquitous television detective programs. The sequence is always the same. Separate the accused, find each party's self-interest, and inevitably they will betray each other.

Over the centuries other famous betrayers also had their co-conspirators. John Wilkes Booth did not act alone in his plot to kill President Lincoln and attempt anarchy. He deceived some of his friends, but others had a similar hatred.

Today, most who betray their spouse enlist persons who were common friends of the couple or other associates in their betrayal. The friends' role is to keep the victim in the dark and propagate lies to other persons mutually known. Unfortunately, this role is sometimes played by divorce attorneys who disparage the victim's character in order to win a better settlement for their client, and in the end profit themselves.

Sometimes the co-conspirators just remain quiet and refuse to expose the betrayal to their mutual friends. They claim it was none of their business and refuse to get involved. Sorry, when you know and still associate with the betrayer and remain quiet, you are a participant and you are giving your tacit approval to the betrayer, while causing additional hurt to the betrayed.

There are many ways the betrayer gets his surrogates to participate in his dirty deed. In the case of Judas, he had the cooperation of the leading priests, the governor, Roman soldiers, and of course the crowds. Betrayal served the agendas of all parties, and so the co-conspirators not only supported Judas's actions, they paid him too. Remember the old adage, "The enemy of my enemy is my friend." But often these friendships are short-lived.

In the case of my alcoholic father, I have no doubt that his barroom buddies knew he was in a cheating relationship, yet none of them told my mother. This despite the fact that most knew her, as we lived in a small town. Perhaps there was a code of silence among drinking friends; perhaps my father had something on each of them. If they told my mother, he would reveal their secrets. I really do not know their motives; however, as I look back on it, his friends also betrayed my mother and our family.

The Betrayer's Deniers

Almost as common as the co-conspirators or the enablers are the deniers. My experience is that when a betrayer has been exposed, his family members and often immediate friends are especially prone to deny his behavior. They just find it very difficult to believe that one of their siblings (or other family member) could become such a person. Remember this is not about behavior, it is about character. So, do not be surprised if you find them turning on you, if you are the one who exposed the betrayer. I know; I have been there. And if you were friends of another family member (members) you may lose them as friends. Even though they may have no part in the betrayal they may feel tainted by their family member. Most likely it will never be the same again between the two of you. The old adage "Blood is thicker than water" often runs true here.

Why These Traits?

I could write another book about why a person might display these negative traits as opposed to more positive ones. Why does one person become more self-actualized, as Abraham Maslow described, and another less so?

We'll likely never know all the reasons, but it is very common, almost universal, that behind every betrayer is an early life of rejection, betrayal, abuse, abandonment, etc. Shostrom, whom I quoted earlier, says there are five reasons a person manipulates.[3] The person:

- Does not trust others
- Is trying to be loved
- Feels powerless
- Is avoiding intimacy
- Needs to be approved of by everyone

Dr. Shostrom highlights the contrast between someone who exploits people and a person who doesn't. "The person who exploits people as though they were things loses the capacity to enjoy intimacy and love in relationships."[4]

Contrast that with the person who desires to self-actualize. "There will become real travail for anyone who desires to become a genuinely actualizing person. But there will be real joy too—*the joy of being what one is and becoming more of what one can be.* This involves risk, faith, vulnerability, and adventure."[5]

While there are many different terms used to describe self-actualized people, I believe that they can be summarized as honesty, awareness, freedom, trust, and compassion. Characteristics that, as we've seen, are in short supply among those who betray.

The Judas Traits

As you look back through the traits we've described in this chapter, you can put the name *Judas Iscariot* next to many of them. When you read the New Testament accounts of Judas, you can see that from the beginning of his relationship with Jesus, he had all the markings of a betrayer. So then, you may ask, "Why did Jesus pick him?" or even, "How could someone like Jesus get fooled by Judas?" I have no doubt that Jesus knew who he was and what he would do. And chose him anyway.

I do know that the next time you experience the horrible pain of betrayal, you need to remember that you are not unique. Jesus—the one in whom even the courts could not find any fault—experienced the worst of all betrayals, one that resulted in his own death. He did not deserve his betrayal, and neither did you.

Many years ago, when I was a pastor and doing graduate studies in counseling and sociology, we were required to undergo therapy with one of our lead professors. As I entered my session one day, I was not in a good mood. My professor asked what was going on and I explained something about someone being destructive and undermining me. He said, "Who in the world do you think you are anyway?" And then he did the therapist pause.

Of course, I had to say, "What do you mean?"

He replied, "Don't you know they even crucified the innocent Jesus?"

Obviously, this is a lesson I have never forgotten. Now I want to pass on my professor's piercing question. How are you going to answer his question, "Who do you think you are anyway?" Don't you know your friends and family members have also been betrayed at some time?

When you have been betrayed and experienced the horrible emotional pain of betrayal, only you can answer how you will deal with the pain.

Points to Ponder

1. Which of these traits does my betrayer have?

2. Which of these traits am I most vulnerable to?

3. What is my constructive plan to keep from being betrayed again?

Chapter 3

Rejection or Betrayal?

Often it is difficult to distinguish the difference between rejection and betrayal. Rejection is more common and quite different from betrayal. While rejection is a part of betrayal, betrayal is typically crueler and more calculating than rejection.

To me, the easiest way to define rejection is when someone withholds from you something you want that they could provide. It could be something such as not letting you into a parking place or refusing to give you affection. Whereas betrayal is when someone plots or has a secret and they use it against you, unknowingly to you, when you were expecting them to be a friend. **The core is they violate your trust in them.**

Both betrayal and rejection are painful when we are on the receiving end. None of us likes either one. But don't let your level of emotional pain be the factor that helps you decide whether you are being betrayed or being rejected.

Even if you have experienced both multiple times, it may be difficult to determine if your current situation is primarily rejection or betrayal. It's best to set aside your first emotional reaction and consider the facts. And this may be very difficult to do. Or possibly you will need an objective friend or a therapist to help you determine what just happened to you.

Why is it important for you to understand the difference between betrayal and rejection? Because if it is betrayal it will help you understand the betrayer personality, and you will be less likely to be deceived again.

Be aware that the more you have experienced either rejection or betrayal, the more difficult it will be for you to sort between them—to be objective and determine the facts. The extreme emotional hurt you are feeling now is likely brought forth by a combination of what has just happened to you and your previous experiences. And you may be fearing what you will lose because of the rejection or betrayal. Whatever happens to us in the present often has some unresolved history in it, which compounds the painful feelings of the current instance of deception and betrayal.

You Can See Rejection Coming

On its own, rejection can be very painful; however, rejection is typically easier to understand and easier to get over than betrayal.

We experience rejection when, for example, another person doesn't want to include us in something they are doing, or they no longer want to have us in their lives. They are trying to make it as easy on us as possible and they do not intend to hurt us. The college rejection letter, the job application denial, employment termination, the refusal to accept a date with us—these are disappointing events and we experience some level of pain and hurt when they happen.

Often the rejecting person is straightforward, perhaps even apologetic. When the romantic partner in your life wants to break off the relationship, they may begin with an apology. The common line is, "It's not about you; it's about me." In a job situation, the hiring manager may say, "I'm sorry, but you do not have the qualifications." Don't you just love it? You know what is coming next when you hear this. It is an attempt on the speaker's part to be honest and minimize the hurt to you. This is not the case with betrayal.

Betrayal is often planned; rejection is sometimes spontaneous and rarely intended to cause harm. Other contrasts between rejection and betrayal are described below.

It's Clearly Over

With betrayal, there is little clarity and much deception, lying, and blame. It seems there is no closure. You are left dangling and wondering, "What happened?"

With rejection, we know it is over—whether it's a relationship, a job application, or a potential date—and we know there is no use pursuing it. Because it's over, we can begin the healing process. Even though we may try to bargain and delay the inevitable, we do know or suspect the relationship is finished.

Because it hurts, we try to minimize the pain by first denying what is happening. Therapists know that in any loss there is the sequence of denial, bargaining, anger, depression, and acceptance. How long we stay in one of these stages or how deeply we feel the hurt does not always depend on what the other person has done to us. It depends on how we see the situation and how the rejection affects our lives.

It's Routine

Rejection is a daily experience—from minor to major issues—for all of us. We experience rejection when the driver beside us refuses to let us in the lane of traffic or when our spouse, parent, or child deliberately turns away and does not listen to us.

The reality of rejection is so predominant that it is a constant in our lives. We even name movies—*He's Just Not That Into You*—after the phenomenon.

It's Noticeable

Rejection ranges from direct behavior such as bullying to passively ignoring us or giving us the silent treatment.

Rejection is sometimes real and sometimes imagined. It is real when we are not picked to join a team, a company, or a college. It is imagined when we get all out of sorts when someone does not call us. Maybe the person forgot, or—as they explain to us later—something beyond their control intervened.

I recall a college student of mine who truly believed that she had a big nose. When she would get on a bus or walk into a room of strangers and she heard laughter but did not know what they were laughing at, she believed they were laughing at her big nose. The fact is that she did not have an abnormally large nose. However, once in her childhood someone close to her had said that she did, and that person laughed at her. From that point on, she equated laughter from strangers with rejection.

Rejection is sometimes toward one person and other times toward a class of people. When it is directed solely at you, it is personal. When it is directed toward a group of individuals you are in, it is typically based on ethnicity, level of education, sex, wealth, or the fact that in some way, you are not like them. While we may believe this is unfair and we may feel hurt, this is the reality of the cruel prejudice in our world. It is commonly recognized among sociologists that prejudice comes from a core of insecurity in the one who is prejudiced against you. We tend to be afraid of people who are not like ourselves, so we label them and find a way to distance ourselves. The more there are of them and the fewer there are of us, the more we are inclined to be prejudiced.

Presently, we are living in a society where if one person sees a person or a group they do not like, they quickly label them *racists*. The motivation behind this is to tear someone or some group down just because they do not like them or the other does not think or act like they do. They are insecure and fearful, so they claim racism when in fact it is more likely than not that the other person just has different views. Is that so terrible?

Rejection can be either overt or covert. It is overt when someone rejects you directly. Perhaps a friend or a romantic partner tells you directly that they no longer want to have anything to do with you. Rejection is covert when the person rejecting you doesn't tell you directly, but their behavior clearly says that they don't want to associate with you anymore. For example, they may not return your texts or calls.

It Requires Little Thought

Tied into our daily experience of rejection is the truth that we accept some rejection as normal and acceptable and give little thought to it. Almost daily we choose the door that says *Men* or *Women*, or we do not park where we see the sign *Handicap Parking Only* and we think nothing of it.

Sometimes we are the one rejecting another, and we can be careless about it. We think nothing of refusing to open the door to a salesperson or hanging up on a telemarketer.

When you must reject someone, do it kindly and carefully. First, because it is the right thing to do. Second, you never know what you may be unleashing in someone whom you are rejecting. News accounts are full of stories of violent outbursts that occurred because someone didn't react well to being rejected.

It is universally recognized that acceptance and belonging are primary human needs. Persons who are constantly rejected or who choose to reject others and therefore do not become part of the social fabric of society may develop a less than healthy emotional profile. We can all share stories of the "weird "or "strange" person who avoids others, peeking out from behind dark curtains, or putting their head down when they pass us. We fail to see that they may have experienced a high degree of rejection, betrayal, loss, or hurt. They may just be trying to protect themselves.

It Is Universal

Many people who are outstanding persons and contributors to society have endured their share of rejection. Here are a few well-known people who overcame rejection and used the experience to form their character.

- Albert Einstein's teacher told his parents that he would never amount to anything.

- Winston Churchill failed the entrance exam to the prestigious Sandhurst twice before finally passing.

- Henry Ford's mother removed him from school at an early age because his teacher said he could not learn.

- G.K. Chesterton, a renowned British author, could not read until he was eight years old. One of his teachers said that if his head were opened, "We should not find any brain but only a lump of white fat."

- Thomas Edison's first teacher described him as "addled;" other educators predicted that he would "never make a success of anything."

- Gregor Mendel, the founder of the science of genetics, attended the University of Vienna but left without graduating. One of his professors observed, "Mendel lacks the requisite clarity of thought to be a scientist."

- Giacomo Puccini's music teacher said he lacked talent and gave up on him.

It's Painful

The level of pain we experience when we are rejected is not determined just by the act of rejection itself. Our pain level is subjective and based on our previous experiences and how we frame the rejection. If we were rejected early in life by a parent, we will be much more vulnerable to a high level of emotional pain when our mate, child, or friend rejects us. We already have a deep wound and now the scab is being torn off the wound. We must deal with the pain of the present and the past simultaneously.

As a therapist, when I counsel someone who is experiencing the pain of rejection, I ask myself if the amount of pain they are demonstrating is consistent with the level of rejection they've experienced. If the painful emotional response greatly exceeds what might be considered a "normal" response, I can be quite certain there is some historical pain that has not been fully dealt with.

If you are the one who was rejected, it is very likely there are times that you will be surprised by the extreme intensity of your feelings and response. Even so, you get to choose whether this experience of rejection will be a building block or a stumbling block in your life.

I am writing this on my birthday. Each year I approach my birthday with deeply mixed feelings. I am grateful to God for my life and longevity and many blessings. Yet there is a fact that I have to face: the reality that my father rejected me on the day of my birth.

Many years ago, after much prodding to understand my life, I asked my mother about the day I was born. She reluctantly told me that the morning she felt the birth pangs start, she told my father, "Today we are going to have our boy." She said "boy" because she wanted a son even though at that time there was no way for her to know the gender of her baby.

Father said, "I am going squirrel hunting," and promptly left. He did not take my mother to the hospital to have me. That is how my relationship with my father started and it never got better. Nor did he change. He betrayed and rejected my mother, me, and many others multiple times.

Nobody Likes It

You and I are alike in that neither of us likes to be rejected. My undergraduate degree is in theology from a private accredited college. When I walked into the dean's office of a state-funded graduate school to enroll in their graduate program, he rejected me, saying that it was his personal belief that an undergraduate degree in theology was not a viable degree even though it was from a qualified college. I did not take kindly to his personal bias and rejection, so I talked to a vice president of the university who assured me I would be admitted. A few days later, I received my letter of acceptance. I was not willing to accept the dean's biased rejection.

I recall a situation (pre-cell phones) in which a husband was a bit late in picking up his wife for a counseling appointment. She had been waiting on a perfectly safe street corner. When she got in the car, she was extremely irate—almost out of control. Obviously, it turned into a big argument in my office. Upon questioning, she revealed that as a child, her father had once been quite late picking her up. She had been left standing on a street corner in a less-than-desirable environment and had become terrified, but she could not safely tell her father that she was scared. This early childhood experience was triggered many years later in an unexpected way with unexpected intensity.

On another occasion a young lady I had been counseling had worked through most of the pain of sexual abuse from her father. Shortly after getting married, she was at the kitchen sink when her new loving husband came up behind her and put his arms around her. This triggered an extreme reaction that neither she nor her husband understood until we uncovered that before sexually assaulting her, her father would come behind her, just as her husband unwittingly had done.

It Generates a Reaction

It's our reaction to a *perceived or actual relational rejection* that affects us the most. It's not so bad when we haven't developed a bond to the person who is rejecting us. However, when we perceive that we do have a relationship and we are rejected, we tend to react in less than positive ways. Some people show their disappointment dramatically and others try to brush it off like it does not matter. Both are methods of trying to deny how much the rejection hurts.

Many years ago, my social psychology professor gave a succinct illustration that I still remember. He said that when someone who is engaged to be married wants to break off the engagement, the person being "dumped" has four choices. They can:

- Shoot themselves

- Shoot the other person

- Shoot both themselves and the other person

- Say there are more "fish in the sea" and move on.

Tragically, we've seen my professor's scenario of premarital rejection come true in many other situations, such as in divorce or separation, loss of employment, or being expelled from college or university. The ones we hear about are those who pick one of the first three options. We don't hear about those who are more emotionally mature and pick the better option, to move on.

It Can Sometimes Turn to Tragedy

One final story where rejection turned to tragedy.

I was once a chaplain–therapist in a maximum-security prison. One day I was paged to go immediately to solitary confinement. I was ushered into a small cell to find a man in deep emotional distress pacing the tiny room. He was about 50 years old, a hard-working Portuguese immigrant. At first, he could barely talk. Finally, in broken English, he got the words out: "I just destroyed everything I have been working so hard to build."

Prior to being locked up, he had been working two jobs to give the best to his family. He had told his teenage daughter many times that he did not want her dating a certain boy because he was not Portuguese. The boy was not a bad person; he was just not who the father wanted his daughter to date.

This father came home one day to find his daughter and her boyfriend sitting on the sofa, talking. There was no inappropriate behavior. Impulsively he went into the other room and came out with a shotgun and killed them both. This father could not take the rejection of his authority.

Points to Ponder

1. What are the facts of the situation?

2. How would I answer this question: "What is *really* happening now?"

3. Is my experience one of rejection or betrayal?

4. How is this experience similar to a previous experience in my past?

Chapter 4

Betrayal in the Family

The family is the greatest place for intimate relationships, safety, trust, and joy, and at the same time it is potentially the place of one's greatest emotional and physical hurt and pain. This almost sounds like an oxymoron. The family is the primary place in society where people trust because they are related by blood and close relationships. Typically, we do not form the same kind of strong bonds in the workplace or in the community as we do in the family unless trust in one or more family members has been broken.

In our family, we expect to be safe, open, and honest. We do not expect our family members to be dishonest, deceitful, or to betray us. When it does happen, the family becomes a place of chaos instead of predictable order. When trust in a family member or the family as a unit has been broken, we become very anxious and insecure. Our foundation of security has been shaken and possibly shattered.

When security in the family has been broken at an early age, it is hard—but not impossible—to feel secure as an adult. Unless one finds some good professional help, a person may live with mistrust and anxiety much of their life and wonder why. This seriously complicates finding and trusting a mate, having children, and developing friendships.

Not only is the family to be a safe place for its members; it is, in fact, the foundation for society. The more chaotic, dishonest, cruel, and destructive the family is to its members, the more this is reflected in society. Today, most of us would agree that over the past twenty-five years, the United States has lost much of its civility. This is a direct reflection of what has been happening in the family.

The great psychologist Abraham Maslow taught that the way to self-actualization is from the family foundation. First, we need our physiological needs of food, clothing, and shelter to be met, then safety, security, and predictability. These basic needs are met first and foremost in the family. The family is where trust is to be modeled, taught, and learned.

The family is also to be the place where our psychological needs for belonging and esteem are to be met. It is to be the place of love, nurturing, and encouragement. If it is not, then there will be little or no trustworthiness in individuals and, ultimately, society. Without these core values, society will be weak and destructive.

Nathan Ackerman, considered to be the father of family therapy, says, "A family has a body, a mind, and a spirit. It has a heart that throbs with the pulse of life. Like the individual it has both depth and surface expression, an inner face and an outer face. It builds a façade, like a mask. If we strip away the mask, we can glimpse the inner being. We can enter the stream of conflict experience of the family in depth."[1]

Every family has within it the seeds of both healthy and unhealthy behavior. These seeds will, intentionally or unintentionally, be watered and nurtured to produce each family's respective fruit.

I wonder what kind of family Judas was raised in that he was so self-seeking that he would betray Jesus, the One who befriended and trusted him. What kind of family did he live in that he would take money from the purse of his friends who trusted him?

Betrayal Between Husbands and Wives

The core of any family—healthy or unhealthy—is the husband–wife relationship. When one or both partners are unable or unwilling to build a healthy environment, bad things are going to happen.

A few of the most overt destructive behaviors in a family are incest, infidelity, physical abuse, and alcoholism and drug addiction. These are clear and obvious. Rejection, abandonment, lack of encouragement, and emotional abuse or neglect are less obvious but have an equally powerful negative effect on family members.

By the time we see these obvious or less obvious negative behaviors, the real damage has already been done. Betrayal in the marriage did not start with these behaviors.

Betrayal began when one or both marriage partners violated their vow to "love, honor, and cherish until death do us part." Once the vows are broken, other destructive elements are unleashed.

Frequently, the betrayal begins in the mind of one person long before it becomes obvious. The old saying, "As a man thinks in his heart, so is he," describes the truth that we humans become what we dwell on. It has also been said, "You are what you think about."

In my own family story of desertion and betrayal, my father's betrayal did not begin when he left town with his girlfriend. What little I have learned about him is that he was not a nice guy as a teen. He was heavy into alcohol and was selfish and abusive. Early in my parents' marriage, he betrayed his marriage vows to his wife (my mother) and his children. His rejection of me and his betrayal of his vow were apparent the day I was born.

Adults who betray their mate not only betray their spouse but also many others, including their children, their parents, and other family members and friends. There is no such thing as a betrayal that hurts only one person. For example, when my father betrayed us, it had a very painful effect on his mother (my grandmother) and her relationship to him.

The effects of the betrayal can impact more than one generation. Betrayal is generational, and it can model a lifestyle that one's descendants follow as well. (More will be said about the generational impact in Chapter 5.)

Separation or divorce makes obvious a betrayal that had begun long before. The vows have been broken. As a therapist who has worked with many broken marriages, the children are now vulnerable to all sorts of abuse and neglect. Now the war is on to see who gets the kids (as if they were nothing more than an old rug). The children may become the victims of neglect and abuse to various degrees. Sometimes they are used as pawns to fight the other parent.

Infidelity

One does not have to be a marriage counselor to know the world is full of marital betrayal. Unfortunately, many of you have experienced the Judas Kiss from someone you loved and trusted. If you have been a victim, it is my purpose to help you understand what happened, grow from it, and become a better person because of it. That is why "Growing Beyond Betrayal" is a good subtitle for this book.

If you are one of the fortunate people who has never experienced this deep pain, I hope this book will be helpful to you as you help your friends through their times of betrayal.

The wound of betrayal is very deep and though it may heal over time and become less painful, there will usually be a sore spot. The feelings of hurt, anger, guilt, or shame lurk below the surface for a long time. Sadly, there is no such thing as complete healing when someone you have been intimate with betrays you. Even so, this does not mean you have to be an emotional wreck all your life or suffer in silence. Chapter 12, "Overcoming the Pain," and Chapter 13, "Growing Beyond Betrayal," will help you recover and live a full, healthy life. There is hope and you can overcome the debilitating pain, hurt, and anger.

When anyone betrays you, the hurt is often beyond description. Many have been heard to say, "It hurts so badly I cannot even describe it."

Though you may not have been formally married to someone, if you have been sexually intimate with another person, their betrayal has a strong impact on your inner core just as though you had been married.

You have probably heard it said many times at weddings that God ordained that the joining of two people would forever unite them. You may not believe what is being said—you may even see yourself as an atheist—but this does not change God's design for humankind. Your belief or lack of belief in gravity doesn't change the fact that it exists, and that you will die if you attempt to defy it by jumping off a ten-story building with nothing to break your fall. So it is with sexual intimacy. You may not see a physical consequence, but that does not mean there is no emotional one. Emotionally, there are many victims of betrayal who suffer silently with guilt and shame, which often morphs into great anger at themselves and the betrayer, followed by depression or self-abuse. This has a great impact on the mental and physical health of the individual.

If you doubt the powerful impact of betrayal on someone who has been betrayed by their intimate partner, just spend one day in a therapist's office and listen. Or listen closely as a friend tells you their story. Or possibly listen more closely to your own heart and soul and don't block out the pain.

The fact is that once we have been sexually intimate with another person, we are changed forever. As the old saying goes, you can only be a virgin once.

If you doubt what I am saying, read this true story from a former client of mine.

When I was 17, I met my best friend, soul mate, and love of my life. Phil and I dated for three years and married. I loved him totally, and I loved being married. I was sure nobody else felt the way we did. After struggling with many years of infertility, our son was born. A year later, Phil was out of work, and we dealt with years of financial problems. But we were a team, and our marriage was strong. I believed we could get through anything.

One night just before Christmas when our son was 10, I received a disturbing phone call from a man who said Phil was having an affair with his wife. I didn't believe it and called Phil at work to warn him that someone was making false accusations. His indifferent reaction unnerved me, so I persisted asking him questions. He finally admitted to the affair. I was shocked and devastated. He asked for my forgiveness, and since I could not imagine life without him, I forgave him. For a year, I reacted with tears and anger if I even thought he was looking at another woman. I eventually found peace, and our relationship moved forward. Or so I thought.

Ten years later, I discovered he was having an online relationship with a woman in another state. I finally realized he had a serious problem, and we went to marriage counseling. The counselor said we had a strong marriage and just needed a "tune up." Another year of my jealousy over perceived threats followed.

Life seemed almost perfect until a few months ago when he became distant after two overnight "business" trips. I confronted him, and he said he'd been having an affair with a woman he met on the internet. It had been going on for nine months. What was different about this affair was his emotional involvement. He said they were in love and wanted to live together. He moved in with her two days later. Before he left, I asked him if there had been others. The look on his face confirmed my suspicions. This was a way of life for him.

Life is slowly returning to normal for me. I have a wonderful support network of family and friends. I still struggle knowing I spent 44 years with a man I really didn't know. I've come to realize there wasn't anything I could have done to save our marriage. He's broken, and I can't fix him. I'm still angry at him for hurting me, our son, and our grandchildren. I have trouble praying for him. Maybe in time I can forgive.

Our news is full of revelations of serial sexual betrayers who are considered competent and accomplished men and women in society. We seem to be shocked every day with a new revelation of bad behavior from someone we admired. While it is the high-profile people who come to our attention, don't be deceived; most betrayal happens to what we call average people in typical marriages. Often where you would least expect it.

I have participated in my share of marriage counseling where there has been some form of betrayal and it is very difficult to restore the marriage and sometimes impossible. In one case the husband was caught in an affair and said he had ended it. In the counseling session I asked if he wanted his marriage and if he was willing to work on rebuilding trust. He responded with a weak yes. I truly doubted his response.

When I said, "Then daily you need to give your wife your cell phone and let her see who you called and check in with her frequently," he refused, got up, and walked out of my office. Though his words were a weak yes, his behavior was a strong "no". Even his statements saying he wanted to fix the marriage were words of betrayal. Obviously, the marriage was over because he was unwilling to be honest.

While it seems in our society that men are the only sexual betrayers in a marriage, that is certainly not the case. According to The Institute of Family Studies: "In general, men are more likely than women to cheat: 20% of men and 13% of women reported that they've had sex with someone other than their spouse while married."[2]

However, "this gender gap varies by age. Among ever-married adults ages 18 to 29, women are slightly more likely than men to be guilty of infidelity (11% vs. 10%). But this gap quickly reverses among those ages 30 to 34 and grows wider in older age groups. Infidelity for both men and women increases during the middle ages. Women in their 60s report the highest rate of infidelity (16%), but the share goes down sharply among women in their 70s and 80s. By comparison, the infidelity rate among men in their 70s is the highest (26%), and it remains high among men ages 80 and older (24%). Thus, the gender gap in cheating peaks among the oldest age group (ages 80+), a difference of 18 percentage points between men and women."[3]

Lest we be inclined to think that men do most of the betraying, don't be deceived by inaccurate societal beliefs. Deeply ingrained in our society are two incorrect beliefs: (1) that men cannot be fully trusted because they are sexually driven and can easily violate their marriage commitments, and (2) that women are more loyal and faithful and rarely succumb to relational infidelity. The fact is men and women are equally capable of betrayal.

I am reminded of one situation in which the wife had an ongoing relationship with a much younger man who was a friend of the family. For years she schemed and lied about the relationship and frequently made disparaging remarks about her husband to her children and their social circle. After she had everything in order as she wanted, she made her exit and received considerable sympathy and support from her social circle. She was so masterful at scheming and calculating that even when she went to live with her male friend, her friends were all convinced it was only a friendship. This was female betrayal with considerable calculation.

What about emotional infidelity? An emotional affair occurs when one partner directs a lot of their physical or emotional energy, time, and attention toward someone other than the person they are in a committed relationship with to the point that their partner feels—and is—neglected. An emotional affair may include long phone calls, long lunches, or sharing of all personal, confidential feelings. Many physical affairs start as emotional affairs and then progress to a physical relationship.

Nonsexual Betrayal

In our society it seems that much of the marital betrayal is sexual because it gets most of the press. However, there are forms of marital and family betrayal where there is no physical contact between two people.

It is all too common for parents to abandon, betray, or reject their children because of their own dysfunction. Sometimes parents do or say things that are very harmful to their children, whether those children are young or adults. When the child pushes back and expresses their feelings, the parent turns against them and rejects them for life. This, in my view, is a despicable behavior on the part of the parent. Parents, you brought these children into this world and have a responsibility to always treat them with respect rather than allow them to be overcome by your own dysfunction. This is much more about your behavior than your child's.

Pornography

Men, since you are the primary users of pornography, I am going to speak directly to you in this section. And women, you can also learn from this section. Contrary to what society tries to tell us, pornography is not an innocent, victimless behavior. It is as significant a betrayal of your spouse as sleeping with another woman. You promised in your marriage vows to be faithful only to her. Lusting after another woman is very disloyal to your wife. You are already breaking down your marriage and planting the seeds for complete future marital breakdown. Is that why you are seeking pleasure vicariously?

When you spend much of your internet time viewing pornography and being sexually aroused by women who are not your partner, you are destroying your relationship. You may find it difficult to see this as an affair, but it is. You think you are not hurting anyone, but you are.

I had a client once who came to me for counseling because her husband was constantly on the internet looking at pornography. The computer was in their bedroom, so their children did not see what he was watching. But often, he would look at pornography late into the night while she was trying to sleep just a few feet away. Men, do you think that husband was respecting his wife and strengthening their marriage?

Parents Betraying Their Children

Although we might like to think otherwise, parents betray their children. They betray their children by violating the values they are trying to teach, by abandonment either emotionally or physically or both, by making career or money of primary importance, just plain day-to-day neglect, by failing to keep their promises and commitments, and by their own abdications, all of which makes them less effective as a parent. Sexual abuse, physical abuse, or fighting over children in a divorce in a way designed to alienate a child from the other parent is also betrayal.

Sexual Abuse

Sexual abuse of a child or adolescent of any age at the hands of a family member is one of the most destructive things one can experience. As we said earlier, a child expects to be safe in their home. All forms of abuse are terrible, but sexual abuse is the worst because not only is trust broken, but when the abuse is sexual it cuts deeper into the psyche than anything else. Even the perpetrator knows it is a very destructive thing to do because they do it in secret and threaten the child not to tell.

The terrible fact is that about one out of every four females and one out of every five males will in some way be sexually abused. Far too often the abuse is perpetuated by a family member. When trust is broken in this manner by someone the victim respects, the victim has a very difficult time getting complete healing. They learn to live with the deep pain; however, it still comes out in another form such as shame, fear, depression, anxiety, or inability to bond.

Sexual abuse is betrayal at the highest level. No society has ever sanctioned it because it is recognized to be a supreme violation of another person.

There are two unique results of sexual abuse. The first is the sense of guilt and responsibility on the part of the victim, even though sexual abuse is **never their fault.** The second is that often the child's (or by now, adult's) anger is not just directed toward the abuser but also at the other parent because they believe the parent knew about the abuse or should have known but did nothing to protect them.

Emotional Abuse

While sexual and physical abuse are clearly forms of abuse, so is emotional abuse. Emotional abuse is the unseen destruction of self-esteem. It imprints deep scars on the inner being, which are the result of many put-downs, screaming, and any other form of verbal assault. It is so common that most therapists have observed this in many of those who come for counseling.

It is the cause of much depression, anxiety, and fear to achieve, especially when the abuse happens to a child. We know that children are keen observers of their environment. The problem is they are poor at accurately interpreting situations.

For example, a father comes home angry and yells at everyone. The child interprets his behavior as, "There is something wrong with me." What the child does not know is the father had just been fired from his job or got a speeding ticket coming home.

When I lived in a condo in Toronto, Canada, I could frequently hear the woman next door scream at the little girl, "You are a dirty little rat." I had gotten to know this couple and believed them to be good people. The little girl was the couple's first child and the mother felt overwhelmed with the challenge of raising a toddler in the midst of the "terrible twos." (I greatly dislike this term; I only use it to make a point. I believe they are the "creative twos.") Because I had developed a relationship with them, I was able to talk to the father alone and explain my concern. He was gracious and soon the verbal abuse stopped.

We are familiar with being on the receiving end of a put-down or being yelled at; each time it happens it affects our self-esteem and confidence. The majority of us could quickly give a story of some hurt we still carry from someone's wounding words. Part of the parental problem is we tend to raise our children just as we were raised. And the amazing thing is that how we have experienced abuse is what we *tend* to do to our children regardless of our resolve to be a better parent.

Parental Alienation

Parental alienation is a behavior many of us have seen, but only recently has it been clinically recognized. Parental alienation is a devious way of depriving a child from having access to or a positive relationship with the other parent. It is the horribly destructive behavior of one parent turning the child or children against the other parent. It is more common in a separation or divorce but can also be done when the family is living together. This usually is a slow, manipulative "brainwashing" behavior where an adult (usually a parent) convinces the child that the other parent is a very bad person to the point the child now hates the alienated parent and ultimately refuses to have any contact. The child's hatred (or fear) of the other parent may prevent the noncustodial parent from seeing the child in spite of a court order granting visitation.

Not only does the alienating parent block the child's normal relationship with the other parent, they also commonly block or poison the child's relationship with the grandparents or other family members.

Why would a parent do this to a child? The bottom line is they are very angry at the other parent and see this as one way they can make the other parent suffer. Also, the alienating parent sees themselves as saving the child from the "terrible

other parent." They can no longer stand the person they greatly dislike and are divorcing, and they believe the child should
feel the same.

Typically, the alienating parent has some deep or obvious
personality issues of their own. In my own practice, I have
seen everything from severe fear of abandonment and insecurity to borderline personality disorder.

The behavior that was evident between spouses in a marriage repeats itself in cases of parental alienation, this time
between parent and child. In fact, each person continues to
be more like they were in the marriage, only now to a greater
degree. So, a woman who was manipulative in her marriage
continues to try to manipulate the relationship between her
ex-spouse and their children. A man who was angry and con-
trolling in the marriage is equally (or more) so as he tries to
control the relationship between his children and his ex-wife.

The alienating parent is completely ripping the family
apart, to the point that the family will rarely even be cordial to
one another again. Sometimes the alienating parent will pick
only one of the children to use against the other parent, and
this creates major conflict and division among the siblings.

It is not just about keeping a child from seeing the other
parent. It is also about poisoning the child against the other
parent. This creates negative—and potentially lifelong—consequences for the child, such as a poisoned view of life resulting in low self-esteem, less ability to bond, and decreased
ability to have a great marital relationship of their own.

The severe effects of parental alienation on children are
well-documented—low self-esteem and self-hatred, lack of
trust, depression, and substance abuse and other forms of addiction are widespread, as children lose the capacity to give

and accept love from a parent. Self-hatred is particularly disturbing among affected children, as children internalize the hatred targeted toward the alienated parent, are led to believe that the alienated parent did not love or want them, and experience severe guilt related to betraying the alienated parent. Their depression is rooted in feelings of being unloved by one of their parents, and from separation from that parent, while being denied the opportunity to mourn the loss of the parent or to even talk about them. Alienated children typically have conflicted or distant relationships with the alienating parent also and are at high risk of becoming alienated from their own children. Baker reports that fully half of the respondents in her study of adult children who had experienced alienation as children were alienated from their own children.[4]

In my own experience, I've seen that when a mother is the alienating parent, the courts rarely hold her in contempt as she manipulates the process. In my opinion, this is because some judges have a hard time believing that a mother would do such a thing. And many of the women are very persuasive to the court and others.

Parental alienation is so destructive to the normal development and maturation of a child that a child may never fully recover from it. All too commonly, once a child is alienated from a parent, they will likely go for years, if not their entire lifetime, separated from a parent who loves them. They can go through life with a big, empty, emotional hole in their heart.

If a child does eventually have contact with the alienated parent, it is not uncommon for the child to betray that parent. Betrayal comes in the form of disrespect, not trusting, borrowing money and not repaying, telling lies about the parent, verbal or physical abuse, and manipulation while physically giving the Judas Kiss. The bottom line is, as a child, they were taught not to trust or respect the other parent. This is a very difficult if not impossible hurdle for them to overcome as an adult.

Assuming the other parent is a decent person, denying one's child from having full and open communication and affection from the other parent is clearly a form of child abuse. It is emotional deprivation. All competent psychologists and therapists would agree that a child needs a healthy relationship with both parents. The reality is both a father and a mother each give unique nurturing to the child, just as grandparents make a unique contribution to a child's development that neither parent can.

One of the problems today is that many attorneys and judges do not understand the symptoms of parental alienation. Many do not understand the needs of a child in their developmental stages because most are trained in law and not child development or family dynamics. This, in turn, results in a form of abuse—that of a parent being abused by not having appropriate time with or access to their child.

The emotional pain the alienated parent experiences is beyond description. Parents who love their children are helpless to rectify the situation. I have observed the deep pain and suffering of a parent who is being deprived of a relationship by an alienating parent. It is a pain as great as, if not greater than, the pain of divorce. Much of the time, parental alienation occurs simultaneously with the separation or divorce. But not always, as the alienation may start when the couple is still together, but the marriage is breaking down. It is emotional pain compounded with more emotional pain.

If you or a friend are encountering this problem, get professional help from a family therapist who is experienced in parental alienation. (Not all are.) There is also peer support available online through groups such as the Parental Alienation Study Group (www.pasg.info or https://www.facebook.com/ParentalAlienationStudyGroup).

Parents, remember that you made a commitment to love, encourage, and properly discipline your children and support their health and emotional growth in addition to providing the basics of proper food, clothing, and shelter. To fail in this is to betray your oath, but more importantly, it is to betray your children.

Alcoholism

I cannot close out this section on parental betrayal without mentioning the effect of alcoholism and drug addiction on young lives. The world is full of adult children of alcoholics (ACOAs); there is even a great worldwide association (https://adultchildren.org/global-fellowship/).

One of my favorite authorities on this subject is Dr. Janet Woititz, who wrote *Struggle for Intimacy*. Here are a few of her phrases that I believe get right to the heart of the issue:[5]

A very large percentage of you grew up in chemically dependent households ... you probably have no idea how to develop a healthy marital relationship.

Ever wonder why you are attracted to that person who is warm and loving one day, and rejecting the next? The challenge to win the love of the erratic and sometimes rejecting person repeats the challenge of your childhood. You are grateful when the inconsistent person throws you a crumb but get bored with the one who is available all the time. (p13)

As an adult, do you find yourself drawn to partners who are both extremely dependent and highly critical? (p. 15)

So, you learn how to not want so that you don't get disappointed. (p. 16)

If any of her words strike a chord with you, read her books and join an ACOA group.

Betrayers and alcoholics are similar. Their behavior affects many people, too many to count. Because my alcoholic father betrayed and deserted our family, I too am a victim of his behavior. While we may learn to live with it, it is a part of our adolescent development. And I to this day can feel the pain of this when I sense someone is rejecting or betraying me, even though they may not be. It is the extended impact that an alcoholic has on his children.

Another thing I learned early in life is that the narcissistic alcoholic is not very good at telling the truth or fulfilling his commitments. Many times, over many years as a therapist, I have had to help my clients forgive and learn to trust.

Can Trust Be Rebuilt?

I cannot emphasize enough that marital betrayal in any form is very destructive to the spouse of the betrayer and is deadly for the marriage. The betrayer may appear to get away with it; however, the betrayer pays a deep moral price that likely will scar their character. When this happens multiple times, the betrayer can become cold, hard, and insensitive to everyone. Sadly, but likely, they will continue to repeatedly betray many others, including themselves.

Marriages and intimate relationships are built on trust. When trust is fractured or shattered, it is very difficult—but not impossible—to repair. If the betrayer is a serial betrayer, the possibility of rebuilding the relationship is much less likely until the betrayer first deals with his or her character flaw.

The word *genuine* is an ancient Greek word that means "without wax." Wax was used to cover up flaws in a vase before an artisan painted over it, so the flaws would not show, and it could be sold as a valuable piece. In marital betrayal, the betrayer uses a variety of methods to deceive their partner into thinking they are genuine. Sooner or later, the flaws in the character become evident.

Regardless of one's professed values, betrayal is a deep moral wound to both the one betrayed and the betrayer.

I do not believe that many parents intentionally set out to harm the children they bring into the world, although I have seen a few who intentionally taught their children unhealthy behaviors. I do believe that all of us have come from dysfunctional families, some more so than others. Because no parent or parents are perfect we have learned both healthy and unhealthy behavior patterns, and we tend to carry these into our marriages and child-rearing.

And of course, all of us add our own dysfunctions to mating and parenting. Some accept their dysfunction and try hard to do better than their parents. Others are clueless as to their ways and have little interest in learning better ways. I never cease to be amazed at men who are avid readers of sports articles and can quote years-old stats but have never taken the time to read a book or article on how to be a better parent.

Among the most difficult things you will ever do in your life are building a strong marriage and being a good parent. And among the most rewarding experiences you can possibly have are working hard to overcome your family's challenges and enjoying the rewards of truly great family relationships.

Betrayal of Parents by Children

Yes, teens and adult children can betray their parents. Unfortunately, this is more common than one may think. It begins with disrespect and verbal abuse and can ultimately end in death.

A few examples of how children betray their parents is by lying about them, stealing from them, not honoring their commitments to them, and not staying in touch with them. There are many more.

No matter how abusive or rejecting your parent or parents have been, being angry at them for a lifetime is more destructive to you than it is to them. Remember, all parents—including you—have their weaknesses. I also know that really bad parents have their own demons to fight. Unfortunately, their children get caught up in that battle.

When counseling adults with unresolved issues with their parents, I help them take a long, deep look at what their parents' situation was growing up or as an adult. The goal is not to cast dispersion on the parents or grandparents, but to help the client understand the challenges they have had. Invariably my clients will find that one or both of their parents had some very difficult and unhappy times in their life. When my clients see this, their anger frequently turns to compassion.

I have often advised young women who are dating or looking for a spouse to check out how the man they are dating treats his mother. This is a clear indication of how he will see and respect her and other women in his life. A man who genuinely loves and respects his mother is usually a good man.

When parents who have loved and sacrificed for their children are disrespected, rejected, betrayed, and abandoned, they experience deep emotional hurt that they find difficult to comprehend. And how can they talk about it to their friends? So, it is worse than a death. They rarely get completely over the betrayal, even when they have forgiven their child, because the fact is there is no such thing as "forgive and forget." The mind is constantly recording everything we see or hear. We may find some healing, but often at the most inopportune time that old memory comes rushing back, delivering much of the same old pain.

Many of these disrespectful children have not had any contact with their parents for many years. In fact, one report I read stated that one out of every four adults has not seen a family member in ten years. Some parents do not even know if their child is dead or alive. I know a senior adult who had several siblings living in the same town. They did not have contact with one another for years. One day he said he had just read his brother's obituary in the paper.

Many parents carry their secret, deep pain into their social worlds, where no one knows their situation. This is a great tragedy in the family where expectations are that one be kind, respectful, and loving to one another and especially to one's parents.

Some of you will protest and say that your parents are not worthy of your respect. If you really are the great and wonderful person you claim to be, you will understand their limitations and forgive them. I am certain you have your share of imperfections.

As a teen I was very angry at my father for betraying and deserting us. Because he abandoned us, my mother had to work six days a week. In college I became very aware of my anger and I realized I had to deal with it. Being a brash 19-year-old, I showed up at my father's home in Miami unannounced. After spending a few days with him, I saw that he was a pitiful, narcissistic alcoholic. I suddenly realized what life would have been like had he stayed in the home with us. And I walked away free.

Betrayal of Siblings by Siblings

I can still remember hearing the teenage girl yell repeatedly at her brother: "You are an illegitimate bastard! I wish you had died the day you were born." I was asked to stop her tirade because, sadly, her parents were too weak to stop this abuse.

Next to expecting safety and trust from our parents, we expect it from our siblings because we are bound together as family. Unfortunately, sometimes the family is not safe because the parents do not model respect and so they don't require the siblings to treat each other with respect.

The abuse by siblings—which can be verbal, sexual, or physical—can have an effect as serious as parental abuse if the parents do not stop it.

I recall reading long ago and have passed the information on to many families that a clear sign of a healthy family is when siblings can rejoice and celebrate with another sibling who has an achievement.

On the other hand, when you see a child seriously acting out, the child is telling us that something very painful is going on in his or her life. The old saying is always true, "Children *show* us how they feel; they don't tell us with words."

Leo Tolstoy, in his novel *Anna Karenina*, wrote this statement: "Happy families are all alike; every unhappy family is unhappy in its own way."

Throughout this chapter I have focused on betrayal and abuse in the family context. My purpose is to help you be aware of these behaviors and not repeat them. In Chapters 12 and 13 we will emphasize how to overcome the issues we have learned as children and the mistakes we have made in our lives that affect others. There is hope; keep reading.

The Good Things About a Family

We have spent considerable time talking about betrayal in the family; however, we cannot close this chapter without mentioning that not all families are all bad all the time. Even when our families have been far less than stellar, there are many good things we should remember and appreciate. We are challenged to do this when we confuse the good things about our family with the experiences that are not so good.

In my own case, my father betrayed and deserted us, and things were tough and embarrassing. Yet there were also many good memories. I remember how hard my mother worked six days a week to provide for us. She set a great example of working hard and not complaining. I smile when I think about my sisters who unknowingly taught me about girls and women; and my grandmother, who was special to all of us. As a youth, like many others, I tried to repress my feelings of hurt and shame. Unfortunately, my feelings came out in the form of anger and other not-so-nice things I don't want to talk about. My sisters and I had our little tiffs, and we rarely talked about our situation—our family certainly did not talk about feelings. However, we did have an unspoken agreement to be kind and supportive to one another.

I want to encourage you to look back and recall the good things and happy times and build a list of them. Write them down. I think you will be surprised at how much good you actually received. Remember you did not become so great and wonderful all on your own.

Points to Ponder

1. Happy or good times I remember are:

   a.

   b.

   c.

2. Who are other people in my life who have been affected by this betrayal?

3. What do I know about my parents' early life situations?

Chapter 5

Generational Betrayal

The betrayer does not betray just one person, but multiple generations.

In my case, my father betrayed at least four generations and possibly more. He betrayed his mother and father, his wife and children, his grandchildren by depriving them of the opportunity to know and enjoy their grandfather, and the extended family.

My father's mother was a wonderful godly lady who dearly loved her only son. She was deeply hurt by his behavior. She had done her best to raise him to be an honorable person with strong values. And after my father betrayed us, she did all she could to try to make up for his behavior to my mother, my sisters, and me. And we are grateful for her influence in our lives. However, no one can ever truly make up for the failure of another person.

The effect on our mother was significant. At age thirty-two, she went from enjoying being a mother and a housewife to having to get up at six each morning and catch the bus to work six days a week. We became latchkey kids.

As a therapist who believes in a systemic understanding of the family, we know that no one act by one person is restricted to one person or one generation. Whatever our behavior, be it positive or negative, we are affected by previous generations and our actions affect future generations.

Most all therapists, when working with an individual, will delve into their client's parental and extended family dynamics in order to understand their client better. I am not suggesting that we are the product of our history and have no control over our own behavior. Nor that our actions are predetermined. Many sociological studies have attempted to prove that criminal behavior is predetermined because of the criminal's family and genetic composition. Research has always fallen far short of proof.

However, as human beings, we are all somewhat to significantly influenced by those before us and around us. We need each other and depend on each other, and this is why we are impacted by one other.

In the seventeenth century, the famous English poet John Donne wrote, "No man is an island / entire of itself; / every man is a piece of the continent, / a part of the main" (Devotions 1624). This is so accepted as a truth that it has been quoted down through the centuries.

In the 1970s, the famed family therapist Murray Bowen developed the concept of the "family diagram" and it soon became popular among most clinicians. It was designed to find patterns among the generations, to see how those same patterns are playing out in one's own behavior. Over time some adapted it and renamed it a *genogram*. Today, genograms are used by various groups of people in a variety of fields such as medicine, psychiatry, psychology, social work, genetic research, and many more.

In family systems, we also know that all families have a family secret. A secret is what everyone in the family knows but no one talks about. When the secret is betrayal, we rarely reveal it to others. We may say, "We are divorced," or "Dad left," or some other phrase. For many years I never told anyone, "I have been betrayed," and I doubt you have, if you have been betrayed. It is only in recent years I have used the phrase.

Even when children are not directly told about a betrayal or some other serious parental issue, they are well aware of what is going on in the family. I have conducted many family counseling sessions where I engaged the children. The parents are always shocked to know how much the children know even though they have not been directly told. I recall one young child shocking her parents, who thought they were keeping their pending divorce from her and her siblings. She said in a very matter-of-fact way, "We all know that." Children are very smart and perceptive; do not underestimate them.

Betrayal of any form in a marriage often results in divorce, which is a major hurt to all parties. Therapists recognize that no matter how socially acceptable divorce has become, it is a major disrupter of family cohesion, child-rearing, and personal well-being. It especially impacts a child's emotional development. Common results are feelings of shame, loss, in ability to trust, abandonment, insecurity, inadequacy, anger, depression, and more.

Shame is that deep feeling of embarrassment you have, even though you have not done anything wrong. It creates insecurity, anxiety, and depression and it can linger and limit for a lifetime one's development and happiness. It is much harder to identify than guilt. With guilt, you know you have done something wrong and you are angry at yourself. When it is shame, you definitely want to hide your source of embarrassment from others.

I grew up with my secret of shame, but I could not label it as such, nor could I understand it. Neither did I talk about it. When my high school girlfriend and I were dancing at our forty-fifth high school reunion, we both, for the first time, shared about our deserting fathers. We both had buried our shame. Now we were secure enough to share.

Previously I wrote of my client who for several years had told his wife that his parents were both dead and he did not have any siblings. Remember, the wife was shocked when one of her husband's sisters called her. He was ashamed to tell his wife that he had lied. And the shame and deceit created a greater problem than had he been able to tell the truth from the beginning. I had already been counseling them for marital dysfunction before the issue was revealed. Once it was revealed, he was ashamed that he had hidden the truth from his wife. And he was greatly relieved when it all came out.

All therapists have dealt with clients' issues that are rooted in family betrayal or divorce. Let's not forget that alcoholism and other addictions, and all types of abuse, are a form of betrayal and very disruptive to healthy family life and especially to children. The destructive issues and results can never be overstated. The damage can never be fully measured. The full impact is never seen immediately, and some results may never surface from the deep psyche of the wounded adult or children.

I have seen the original destructive behavior repeated in second and third generations in a shocking way, even when the person had no contact with the original wrongdoer. It is almost as though the person in the second or third generation had been trained by the original betrayer. This shows the longer-term power and effects of the original behavior. This is not an indication of predetermined or predestined behavior. I want to stress this again. However, do not ever underestimate the long-term effects of your behavior or the behavior of another person on your generational family.

Positive Traits

Another way to think about it is in terms of positive traits. Positive traits and behaviors in a family are also passed down generationally.

You get to choose what you want to pass down to your children and grandchildren. Take some time to study your family and identify what positive traits you see being handed down and what negative traits you'd be wise to be aware of and eliminate from your life.

Think carefully when you are tempted to cut off communication with a parent or grandparent. Cutting off can be a form of betrayal. When a person betrays their parents and shuts off contact, they deprive their children access to grandparents who are essential to their children's identity. I have heard far too many clients and social friends say with sadness and emptiness that they never knew their grandparents. They are like adults who were adopted as children, some of whom seek their birth families to regain a sense of their historical identity.

When one is deprived of this historical identity, one may feel like they were dropped onto Earth from the planet Mars.

Broken trust or lack of faithfulness is powerful. Do all you can to pass on only the best traits to your family.

Our grandmother, my father's mother, had a great positive influence on my life and my siblings' lives. Much of the good that I am, and do, I owe to Grandmother's example of how she gave to us and others.

Many years ago in youth camp, as we sat around the bonfire, we loved singing, "It only takes a spark to get a fire going." That is true for both positive and negative traits.

The Role of Trust and Love

Trust in oneself and others is the core that provides the deepest, strongest foundation in an individual. Love and trust are closely aligned. Love is respectful and is generates trust. And trust generates love.

That is why Abraham Maslow and other psychologists place trust as the primary factor in healthy emotional development.

One more point. Sometimes the generational seeds of betrayal or other equally destructive traits are planted long before they grow into full-blossom betrayal. Their source may never be identified.

External Influences

We need to keep in mind that our generational family is not the only influence on an individual. Among other influences, there are education, society and its cultural impact, and one's close friends.

Edwin Sutherland, considered to be one of the most influential sociologists of the twentieth century, developed his highly acclaimed theory of differential association (it sounds like a complex theory, but it is very down to earth) in which he postulated the cause for juvenile and criminal behavior. His core principles state that delinquency is learned from close and frequent contact with a criminal or delinquent and it is an expression of needs and values that are the same as those expressed by non-criminal persons. We are all driven by needs and values. The question is how are we going to try to meet them? Will we do so in a positive, constructive way or in a self-serving way that damages oneself and one's family and society? (For a detailed explanation of the theory, see the Appendix, "How We Learn to Betray.")

We are all going to be greatly influenced by our generational family, friends, and society. I hope you have been given a good foundation of trust and love and that you will commit yourself to passing it on to your family and society. If you were not given that core of being able to trust, I hope you will find a good therapist who will help you build it.

Please take time to carefully review Chapters 12 and 13 on "Overcoming the Pain" and "Growing Beyond Betrayal," where we give specific instructions on how to create a better life for yourself and the generations that follow.

Points to Ponder

1. The first person I knew who really trusted me was _____ .

2. Their trust has affected me in these ways: _____ .

3. I trust _____ and I encourage them by _____ .

Chapter 6

Betrayal by a Friend

Betrayal by a friend is almost as painful an experience as betrayal by family members. There are several similarities between the two.

Many of our friends who end up betraying us already exhibited some of the traits we described in Chapter 2, "Character Traits of a Betrayer." Because they were people we considered to be a friend, we missed or denied the negative clues. We often prefer denial to facing the possibility that we could have chosen a poor friend. Even when family members or friends see what is happening and tell us so, we frequently don't like their advice.

I have a bit of advice I give to my clients and friends who are struggling with a dating relationship and wonder if they should move forward to make the relationship more permanent. My warning is, "The behavior one exhibits in the dating or friendship stage is what they will sooner or later display in the formed relationship."

A friend of mine married a lady he loved and after several years in the marriage she seriously betrayed him by having a relationship behind his back. He had forgotten that she had done this to him twice while they were dating. Like most of us, he ignored the signs and went with the feelings he had for her.

As with family members, you must first have a relationship of trust with a friend before you can be betrayed by them. All friends are not alike in that we trust different friends to different levels. There are social friends who we do not know well and there are intimate friends who we open up our lives to and trust. Go slow but also do not be paranoid about having good friends or you will end up very lonely.

The media, history, and literature are full of examples. If you doubt this, listen to country music for an hour.

More importantly, you have most likely experienced the pain of betrayal and rejection by someone you chose as a friend. Unlike our friends, we do not choose our family members. (They did not get to choose us either.) If they had had a vote, they may not have picked us. I once heard a father say, "I love my daughter, but I would not have picked her." However, she was good for him because she taught him a lot about himself.

When a friend—someone we chose—betrays us, we are more likely to be hard on ourselves for being so "dumb," "blind," "stupid," etc. Much of the time we did not make a poor choice because initially we trusted each other, and the relationship went well. Unless we have foreknowledge of someone being a serial betrayer, it is difficult for us to foresee what might happen. Many friends are friends for a long time, and we have a great time with them until they reject or betray us. If this happens, we need to keep in perspective that we did have many good times. And many friends are friends for a lifetime. A friends betrayal colors all of the past in a negative way because it hurts so much.

The great Russian writer Aleksandr Solzhenitsyn was convinced that "the line of dividing good and evil cuts through the heart of every human being."1 Unfortunately, this is true. We have in our human nature the potential to be true and trustworthy and cruel and distrustful. Welcome to the human race. Remember you are part of it; you too have the same potential to reject and betray. However, I hope you will remain a faithful friend to your friends for life. In fact, on reflection you may have been guilty of betraying a family member or a friend. If so, now is the time to make it right if you have not done so already.

None of this is to say we should excuse betrayal or deny the hurt it brings. We do need to accept the reality of life. Find the middle ground between being a starry-eyed idealist and a doom-and-gloom pessimist. Be a realist and acknowledge this is life. Then we do not need to look at every friend or person with a paranoid view nor lock ourselves away in a closet, nor live in a Pollyanna world, where you think everything is sweetness and light. No one can offer you a life free of physical or emotional pain. Rose gardens are full of thorns.

I once read the statement: "The worst thing about being surprised is you are surprised." While it is impossible for us to speculate why Jesus chose Judas as his friend, I know he was not surprised by Judas's betrayal. In fact, he even predicted it.

Jesus hosted his closest circle of friends for His final meal during the Passover festival. Judas was one of the twelve gathered. During the dinner, Jesus said to the group, "One of you will betray me."

Each person quickly denied it would be him. But Jesus pointed out exactly who was going to betray him. It was the person who dipped his hand in the bowl at the same time Jesus had.

Judas asked, "Surely not I, Rabbi?"

Instead of assuring Judas, Jesus confirmed Judas's statement. Judas was to be the betrayer. Soon Judas got up from the meal and proceeded to complete his act of betrayal.

Later that evening, when Judas entered the garden where Jesus was meditating, Judas said, "Greetings, Rabbi," and kissed him on the cheek.

Jesus replied, "Do what you came for, friend." Friend!

As the old adage goes, "With friends like this, who needs enemies?"

No, Jesus was not surprised.

This is the Judas Kiss. (This is why we have titled this little book *The Judas Kiss*.) It is the kiss of betrayal by one who was considered to be a friend. Remember that Jesus and Judas had spent the better part of three years together. And when Judas betrayed Jesus, he kissed Jesus on the cheek. In the first century, the kiss was revered as a sign of respect and deep friendship.

Have you ever had a friend who, like Judas, was part of your closest circle even while they plotted against you? Did they pretend to be your friend, even when they were confronted with their evil deed? It's happened to me more than once. I once had a couple of colleagues who were friendly to my face. It took me some time to realize that behind my back, they were very disrespectful to me. Although their behavior did not pierce me like my father's actions had, some might call what they did a form of betrayal.

In another situation I had a longtime friend, or so I thought, who enjoyed my trust and hospitality in my home, all the while lying to me about many things I was trusting him to do. When I became suspicious, I told him to leave and severed all ties.

Yes, I have been betrayed more than once by family or friends. Each time it happened, it hurt terribly so I took some time to step back and evaluate the situation. I had a decision to make: would I become closed and stop trusting or continue trusting and know it could happen again? For me, spending the rest of my life not trusting others was not an option. You too have a decision to make. Remember if you decide to close up and not trust, that is not a painless life. It is a lonely life. I hope you will choose to trust but learn to be more vigilant. And know you can overcome the hurt if someone betrays or rejects you.

Being of Scottish descent, I love the story of William Wallace as depicted in the movie *Braveheart*. I love his strength and determination against all odds. However, the sad part of the story is when his fellow countryman, Robert the Bruce, betrayed him to the English, leading to Wallace's defeat and ultimate brutal torture and death. Note that it was his fellow countryman whom he trusted who betrayed him. Yet in spite of the fact that Wallace was betrayed and tortured to death, his faith in himself and commitment to his country still won. Trust, faith, and forgiveness will always win over betrayal and dishonesty. As I have reviewed a bit of the life of Wallace, I would suspect that though the physical torture was beyond horrible—even beyond description—he must have felt great agony and torture in his soul, knowing he had been betrayed by a fellow countryman. One who vowed to be his friend.

Betrayal by a friend can be a deep, indescribable emotional hurt, because we have trusted them with our secrets and confidences. Sometimes we are afraid that we will be emotionally "drawn and quartered" in public by those who say, "I told you so."

David, the king of Israel who wrote many of the Psalms in the Bible, wrote about his agony of betrayal, after he was betrayed by a friend:

> If an enemy were insulting me,
>> I could endure it;
> if a foe were rising against me,
>> I could hide.
> But it is you, a man like myself,
>> my companion, my close friend,
> with whom I once enjoyed sweet fellowship[2]

You have probably heard the expression: a loyal friend sticks closer than a brother. A loyal friend is special and rare. If you have one, you are a rich person indeed, so celebrate it and rejoice and do all you can to cherish and preserve the friendship.

Do you remember Bernie Madoff? He was a corrupt man who ran the biggest Ponzi scheme ever recorded. He cheated hundreds of people out of billions of dollars.

Madoff started his scheme by soliciting his friends, who in turned recruited their friends. Did you know he even cheated his sister? Over how many years and with how many people did he promise to wisely invest their money, all the while he was enriching himself?

Madoff is a clear example of a serial betrayer with no conscience. Not all those who betray are this bad.

Building a trusting friendship takes time. Don't go rushing into a new friendship or intimate relationship with your heart wide open and your eyes and mind closed. And watch out for those who push very hard early on to get you to quickly and completely trust them. The more they push or pressure you, the more dangerous they likely are. And always be on guard for those who want to protect you. They are usually out to control you and will often bring you harm and great emotional pain. And one word of advice: if you want to risk having a falling out with your best friend, either enter into a business partnership with them or loan them money.

I am not cautioning you against having friends. Wonderful, faithful friends are more valuable than rare precious jewels. So rare, in fact, that you will have many social friends but only one or two whom you can completely trust. Enjoy them and be grateful for them. And don't forget to tell them how much you appreciate them.

Points to Ponder

1. What do I think are the traits of a trustworthy friend?

2. What clues help me see that a friend is not trustworthy?

3. Is my personal need to overcome loneliness so great that I am vulnerable to creating friendships with untrustworthy people?

Chapter 7

Self-Betrayal

While being betrayed by a family member or friend is a terrible experience, betraying oneself may even be more destructive and tragic.

When one is betrayed, one can overcome the hurt as I will describe in the following chapters. However, self-betrayal is ordinarily progressive and difficult to reverse, because one can so delude oneself that one is unwilling and possibly unable to see one's own destructive thinking, behavior, and consequences.

Self-betrayal is self-deception, which leads to self-justification of one's behavior, which then permits one to behave in any manner one chooses. Then self-betrayal often leads to one betraying another.

In our environmental, intellectual, and emotional worlds, nothing remains static. Things are either growing and improving or decaying and declining. There may be a short period of time that the growth or decay is not easily seen by the uninformed, but that does not mean it is not there. Have you experienced seeing the growth of a plant or a tree only to see it slowly die in spite of all our efforts to save it? Or did you suddenly one day discover it was already dead?

Have you ever bitten into a shiny apple only to find it rotten inside?

More tragically, we may have seen the slow decline of the morality and behavior of a family member or friend. How many times have you heard the family of a mass shooter say they never saw it coming?

Many times, we do not see the decline. Not because it is not there, but because we do not want or like to see it. So, we tend to deny it until some significant event erupts and rips off our blinders. Then we say, "I just cannot believe what I am seeing," or, "This is not the person I know." And like uprooting a tree or a plant, it may be too late to influence positive change in that person.

When a marriage breaks down or a teen gets in serious trouble, it is never sudden. It just *appears* to be sudden. However, seeds of destructive behavior have been germinating for some time.

One day we wake up and see weeds in our beautiful lawn. They may seem to suddenly appear, but the seeds had previously blown in unknown to us. Over time they germinated, grew, and then became very obvious to our family and friends.

The Significance of Core Values

Most people are raised in families that attempt to teach healthy core values. Some parents are better at this than others; however, I have only on a few occasions seen or heard of a family directly teaching their children antisocial values or behavior. However, each individual will choose to accept or reject the family and societal teachings and values.

Sadly, too often parents get a big surprise when their child grows up and demonstrates unhealthy values that are very different from what the family lives by and tried to instill. Parents search themselves and often feel badly or lose sleep over how their child turned out when they see their child living values that are in serious conflict with their family values or typical social values. As an observer of society and a long-time therapist I have seen this immeasurable times.

Self-betrayal is the violation of the values and ethics one was exposed to from early life on, the values that are commonly accepted in our society, or when one has actually believed in and declared certain values but by one's intentional behavior has significantly or consistently violated them. These values may include espousing fidelity to their mate, protecting their children, and being truthful, yet living a life that is quite the contrary.

I believe we can assume that most everyone in our society has been given some positive core values either by their family or by societal expectations. Frequently victims of betrayal tell me they just cannot understand how their betrayer could do such a thing, considering he or she was raised in a good home by good parents.

A person caught up in self-betrayal may experience severe consequences. When you violate your own principles and values, you may initially be very unhappy with yourself. Our society calls it conscience. However, what we can never truly know is how much one has internalized the healthy or unhealthy values. Therefore, as outsiders we cannot determine how much discomfort or "guilt" one is truly experiencing.

Because even if they are experiencing a fair bit of guilt, it is unlikely they will admit it. It is only when the conscience or inappropriate behavior is seriously disturbing them and becoming so convicting that one may choose to stop and turn one's life around. Or they will blindly continue on until they are completely numb to the results of their behavior and have harmed someone or themselves.

How do you think Judas felt about himself? Likely when he betrayed Jesus, he thought he was doing the right thing. But in the Bible, it implies that Judas must not have foreseen the full consequences of his action. He must not have expected Jesus to be condemned to death, because when he learned that Jesus was going to be killed, he tried to return the bribe he had received for turning Jesus over to the religious leaders. The religious leaders refused to take the money back. Judas, in despair, went out and hanged himself.

This reminds me of Viktor Frankl who said, "Despair is suffering without meaning."[1]

Not all consequences of self-betrayal are so severe. But they can be serious.

The question is, which is more painful for you, betrayal by a family member, betrayal by a friend, or betrayal of yourself? You will probably reply, "It depends."

And that is likely the case. There are many variables but two big differences between betrayal by a family member or friend and betrayal of yourself. When you are betrayed by a family member or a friend you have no control over the betrayal, and you are probably very surprised when it happens. The only control you have is over how you handle yourself in the aftermath. Take a look at Chapter 11, "Your Reaction to Betrayal."

In the case of self-betrayal, you have complete control. You have control over your actions and how you choose to deal with your behavior. In either case, control is a big issue because we like to be in control of what is happening in our lives. This is a bit of an illusion because we typically do not have as much control over our lives as we think we do. We continue to fool ourselves, so we can feel more at peace and less anxious about uncertainty.

Self-betrayal is when you violate the principles and values you were taught by your family, your religion, and society. We are taught these values both by direct teaching and modeling by others. Even at a young age, you learned many of your values by observation. For example, perhaps you saw your sibling lie to your parents, and you observed how they got punished for doing so. Or they got away with it.

So how have you betrayed your own values? We have all betrayed our own values at some level. The question is how, with what frequency, and to what degree? Did you lie, cheat, steal, betray, or be unfaithful in your relationship? What did you do about it?

I recall a situation where the wife was deceiving and lying to others about her husband, to set herself up as the good wife. And she was doing such a good job at it that none of her friends or the couple's mutual friends would have guessed that she was already in a secret relationship. The more she lied the more she was already heading down the road of self-destruction. I followed this case for some time. After she separated from her husband, over a period of years she became an alcoholic and was quite depressed. She has emotionally destroyed herself to the extent that today she has no contact with her children or grandchildren. The only word that fits this situation is *tragic*.

Unfortunately, this is not just one person's life story. I recall reading that one in four adults has not seen a family member in over ten years. I at first questioned this until I began to think of how true that statement is among the people I know.

Human nature is such that once you start down the road of self-betrayal, self-justification, and self-deception, you will most likely continue to sink lower and lower until you take a very serious look at yourself and come to grips with what you are doing. Like the wife in the previous story, you may end up addicted, depressed, and alone. The road of self-betrayal is all downhill and the farther you travel on it, the greater the deterioration. However, if you have "cheerleaders" who continue to tell you what a great person you are, it is unlikely you will change.

We might ask, did Judas betray himself? Judas certainly ended up destroying his friendships and his reputation. Ultimately, he died at his own hand. And his name has gone down in infamy so that now, two thousand years later, we call this little book *The Judas Kiss* and the world associates his name with the essence of betrayal. What a way to be remembered!

Just as I wonder what values Judas held and whether he betrayed himself, I wonder what your values are. Are you betraying yourself? If so, I hope you feel guilty about it and stop your self-destructive behavior. For I would see it as tragic if you could violate your own values without it bothering you. Sadly, there are many who have so numbed their conscience by denial, drugs, alcohol, the drive for money, power, and things that they are unaware of what they are doing to themselves.

Childhood and Values

As a child, your family probably was conscientious about instilling core family and societal values in you. Basic values would include don't lie, don't steal, be kind to your siblings, brush your teeth daily, and many more. Rarely does a family teach their children to lie, cheat, or steal. But I have seen it.

Even though your family taught good core values, it is also very likely that your children did not *consistently* live everything you taught them. That is not unusual because none of us *always* follow the values we teach or profess. We can't. We are human and living our values one hundred percent of the time is impossible. As a child, you carefully watched your family members to see if they were living up to the values they were teaching you and sometimes punishing you for when you didn't follow them. The more *inconsistent* they were in what they taught and practiced, the more confused you became and the less you established your own solid core values. Even though every family displays these occasional inconsistencies, a small number of people lack good basic values and ethics. The problem is, it is easier to know than to act on the values.

Whether you are an adolescent, teen, or adult, there are consequences for violating your own values and principles. The consequences are internal to your own peace of mind. The more conflicted you are between what you were taught about good moral values and how you live, the less likely you will be at peace with yourself.

Some of the consequences of self-betrayal include guilt, anger, anxiety, depression, and just plain unhappiness with oneself. When we violate our values, we also become very good at blaming others for our unhappiness. The more frequently and aggressively I see someone blaming others, the more I am aware that they are probably doing the same internal self-blaming. Or they are so oblivious to themselves they do not have a clue who they are. And they have probably activated one or more of the psychological monkeys.

The Four Psychological Monkeys

There are four psychological monkeys. Have you heard the expression, "I have a monkey on my back"? Guilt, fear, anger, and inadequacy have been called the four psychological monkeys—manifestations of a negative power that controls you, dominates you, or keeps you from being free, happy, and content.

The monkey is notorious for its constant annoying chatter. We want to shut it up, but we can't. It chatters day and night, whether we are alone or with others. We want to shake it, but it is very adept at hanging on and digging its claws into us. It inhibits our movement and freedom. It destroys our relationships because it dominates us.

The Guilt Monkey

Is guilt your favorite monkey? Do you go around feeling guilty or saying how guilty you feel? Does this monkey have a grip on you and control your life? Let's examine it.

The first step to freedom is understanding and acknowledging your monkey. When you understand how your monkey controls you and makes you miserable, then you can learn how to tame it.

Guilt is feeling a sense of remorse for violating society's rules or the personal rules you've set for yourself. There are times when we are guilty but don't have a sense of remorse because we did not know we violated a law. Remember when the police officer pulled you over for running a stop sign that you really did not see? You were guilty even though you did not feel guilty. Contrast that to how you felt when you knew there was a stop sign but you did not stop. You were guilty and possibly had guilty feelings. Most competent police officers can identify a guilt-ridden perpetrator regardless of what the person says.

The capacity and intensity with which we acknowledge and feel guilt is developed in us by the age of six or seven. We are not born with a list of rights and wrongs preprogrammed in our brains. We each learn about right and wrong and guilt from our significant caregivers. Some parents feed a great amount of guilt-inducing statements and feelings into their small children. The child grows up with his heart and mind full of guilt, so he takes responsibility and feels guilty for everything that happens around him. Or he blocks it out and as an adult feels very little guilt.

I know a gentleman that everyone liked, but he would constantly say he was sorry even if he had not caused the problem or even participated in the issue. I truly believe if you had run him over with a truck, he would have apologized for being in the way. As a result, he was a nice person but weak. He would not challenge any significant issue at his workplace.

Early in life we are taught by our parents what to feel guilty about and what degree of guilt we should feel. Sometimes we accept how they are programming us. Other times we reject their teaching because we don't share their sense of guilt. Since no two adults were raised in exactly the same way or taught identical life lessons by their parents, it is common for married couples to get into arguments about feeling guilty.

To illustrate, a wife may say, "I feel so guilty about what happened," and her husband will reply, "I don't."

Then she will say, "How can you be so insensitive?"

Now the war is on. The wife's guilt turns into anger, and the husband shrugs his shoulders and walks away.

In another scenario, a husband may have an affair and apologize, but not express the level of guilt his wife expects him to display. She thinks, "If I did that, I could never live with myself," or, "I would show more remorse than he did, so I guess he isn't sorry. Since he's not very sorry, he will probably do it again."

Watch a mother try to get her little boy to say, "I'm sorry I hit my sister." He may not be sorry. He may be glad he did it. In fact, he may even feel he had good reason to strike her.

Feeling a high level of guilt is one extreme. The other is to never feel or acknowledge guilt. Yes, there are many people in our society—mostly men—who rarely or never have a guilty feeling. When they have been properly evaluated by a professional and it has been determined that they truly feel no guilt, we consider them to have something called *antisocial personality disorder*. People with this diagnosis are sometimes more commonly labeled either a *psychopath* or a *sociopath*.

Typically, people with antisocial personality disorder are very bright, articulate, perfectionistic, manipulative, good-looking, and well-groomed males. Many are professionals. A sociopath or psychopath is rarely a "dirty old man in a raincoat."

In an earlier chapter, I referred to meeting a sociopath in a social setting. He had heard I was working in the prison. He told me that his psychiatrist had diagnosed him as a psychopath. This man was a very successful orthodontist who willingly revealed to me his diagnosis of sociopathy. He told me that he never felt guilty about anything. He stayed out of serious trouble by thinking through the potential consequences of his actions, specifically, what he might lose if he got caught acting on his impulses. He said, "I don't step very far over the line because I don't want to go to jail and lose my great life." He was such a nice person that anyone who met him socially would have liked him.

I will never forget the day I visited an inmate in his solitary confinement cell. I saw him several times a week for several months while he was jailed and awaiting trial for raping and murdering a young boy. The day after he was found guilty and sentenced to life in prison, I entered his cell. He was sitting at his desk with his back to me; I called him by name and asked him what he was doing.

He replied, "Drawing a schematic for a radio receiver."

Although I knew he was a psychopath, I was still shocked. What would you have been doing and feeling if you had just been found guilty of this crime and sentenced to life in prison?

As I pursued the conversation, I asked, "Do you feel guilty for what you have done?"

He replied matter-of-factly, "No. In fact, if my mother came in here now, I could kill her and feel nothing. I only regret what I have done because now I have to spend life in prison and I cannot be out on the street."

I have to admit that I thought, "I am glad you are going to spend life in prison and not be on the street." Recently I saw an article in a Canadian paper where he had applied for parole but had been denied. Great, now he still cannot be on the street to harm someone else.

A big mistake many people make is to assume that others around them feel the same degree of guilt over the same things they do. Chances are that two people don't feel the same degree of guilt or remorse over the same things.

Having a hyperactive (overactive) or hypoactive (underactive) thyroid will put you on emotional highs and lows until you get medication to level it out. Having an overactive or an underactive sense of guilt is not healthy either. You may need to do some work on your guilt issues if guilt is the monkey on your back.

Most mental health professionals will agree that at least ninety percent of our guilt is anger at ourselves for not measuring up to our own values and expectations. Thus, many people with a hyperactive sense of guilt come across as very angry. They are so angry at themselves they cannot contain the anger, so they spew their anger at those around them. Then it becomes a vicious cycle. They feel more guilt because of the way they treated others, which produces more anger at self, which again gets taken out on others.

The cycle continues.

This cycle of guilt is common in people with substance use disorders like alcoholism or addiction. A person feels inadequate or guilty, so he drinks or uses drugs to mask his feelings. Then when he is sober, he becomes aware of how he hurt others when he was drinking or using, and then he feels guilty. He drinks or uses again to mask the guilty feelings.

If you betrayed someone and are carrying guilt for what you have done, there is hope. In Chapter 13, "Growing Beyond Betrayal," I will show you how.

The Fear Monkey

When we betray ourselves or another person, we activate the fear monkey, if we have typical core values. When we live with the fear of being found out—of having our secret exposed—we fear we will be shamed, rejected, or possibly even arrested.

We all have some things we would never want exposed to anyone, even our best friend. The more serious our secrets and the more fear we have of being exposed, the more miserable our lives become. Let's look at how the fear monkey affects us.

Fear is both good and destructive at the same time. It is a natural emotional defense we are all endowed with. Fear keeps us alive every day. It is good to be afraid of walking out into the street in front of an oncoming truck or stepping out of an airplane at thirty thousand feet without a parachute (or even with one). Fear keeps us from drinking out of a bottle labeled with skull and crossbones or putting our hands on a red-hot stove burner. It keeps us from criminal acts because we are fearful of others viewing us in a negative light, or of being caught and going to prison.

But fear that is nurtured and fed grows into a monster that controls and dominates you rather than protects you. Soon the fear monkey is on your back chattering incessantly to be careful, look out, don't trust, and so on. Soon the symptoms consume and control you and make you miserable. Now the fear monkey is in charge of your life; you are not in charge.

Fear can morph into something much larger than what it started out to be. Assume someone becomes terrified of the dark and they nurture that fear. It could grow into a fear of going outdoors, fear of spiders, fear of flying, or even fear of eating, which could become anorexia or bulimia. It could become obsessive-compulsive disorder (OCD). This new creature bears no resemblance to its original source; it becomes much harder to recognize and resolve. This is why we need to address and resolve our fears before they become too difficult to manage and they take over our hearts, bodies, and our lives. We need to identify the monkey while we still can.

Many addictions are rooted in fear. When fear gets triggered, anxiety starts to take over, so the fearful person eats, shops, drinks, snorts, looks at porn, has sex, cuts himself, and so on.

Much of your fear is coming from you trying to hide the truth from yourself and others because you are fearful of what will happen if others learned the truth about you. We all have our "little secrets" that we try to hide from ourselves and others. However, when these become extensive and we begin to obsess over them, we are soon controlled by fear. Have you heard the expression, "I would just die if my friends found out the truth about me"? This person is already dying—internally.

Then there is *imposter syndrome*. Imposter syndrome is when one thinks they are inadequate and they are fearful others will find out, when in reality they are very competent. I recall being asked to do an executive personality assessment on a successful businessman. He truly believed he was an imposter. I showed him all his competency and personality scores, which showed he was much more capable than he had thought true. This revelation set him free and he soon became even more successful and highly recognized in the financial community.

Fear is the mother of anxiety. Anxiety is not an emotion. It is an emotional reaction to fear. When our fear alarm bells go off, they trigger our system to get ready to run or fight. Our body produces adrenaline to give us an abundance of extra energy for protection.

If you don't use up this energy force to run from the "bear" or fight it, you will start to shake and tremble. Your body is not equipped for this type of reaction, in which your body generates adrenaline but never uses it. Your fear is triggered, but you may have to stay at your desk or continue doing some other nonphysical activity. When your grandmother felt anxiety, she could beat the rug with a wire whip, chop a cord of wood, carry buckets of water, or slop the hogs. Today, we are told to go to the gym and burn it off. Few of us do, and as a result, adrenaline eats us up inside and destroys our physical, emotional, and relational health.

I often compare anxiety to starting a car, shifting it into neutral, putting your foot on the accelerator, and pressing it all the way to the floor. You don't go anywhere, but the car shakes and roars. Immediately you hear your father yell, "Don't do that! You'll destroy the motor!" Yet if you were to put the car into gear and accelerate, you would do no harm because you are using the energy.

Humans are masters at converting fear to anger. When your little child runs out into the street, you scream, yell, and grab him by the arm. You may even spank him. You have just converted fear to anger. Others may not see your fear, but they are likely to observe your anger, which came from the fear.

Teenagers don't understand why parents are so angry when they come home much later than their curfew. They try to explain why they were late, but all they get is anger from a terrified parent. Neither the teen nor the parent has a clue that the parent's fear has been converted into anger.

When you have been hurt by someone or by life's circumstances and you hold the emotional pain of that event inside, it is common to become chronically angry. You have chosen to convert your fear into anger to protect yourself from being hurt again.

Anger is your army of defenders, pushed to the frontlines by fear, and now the anger monkey is in charge.

The Anger Monkey

When you hold onto volatile anger to defend yourself, it is like you are wearing an invisible sword in an invisible scabbard on your hip. You know it is there and so does everyone else. When someone starts to threaten you, you rattle your saber and if they don't back off, you pull it out and wave it in the air. At this point most people do back off. However, occasionally there is some "fool" who doesn't see your sword or fails to heed your warning, so you stab him with it.

This whole sequence started because someone betrayed you or you betrayed yourself. You felt the emotional hurt and pain of your self-betrayal and decided you never wanted to feel that way again, so you unconsciously equipped yourself with your sword, and now you are always prepared for battle. You do not want to be exposed to yourself or others.

The persons who get stabbed never know what hits them or why. They go away more confused than anything. You have successfully protected your fear and converted your fear into anger to protect yourself. But there is now a new problem: you have just lost self-control and harmed another friend—or is this person now a *former* friend or a soon-to-be ex-spouse?

Most of us can quickly identify overt anger when it is expressed in obvious ways. These expressions of anger can be mild to extreme. The most common expressions of anger are:

- Verbal expressions, such as screaming, yelling, arguing, verbal abuse, threatening, and the like; and

- Physical abuse including slapping, hitting, punching, or extreme violence such as rape.

While these expressions are serious, and we need to take note of them, there are also many subtle expressions of anger that can be just as destructive. Some people choose less obvious expressions of anger because it is not safe to overtly express their rage. They try to deny their anger and bottle it up, but these expressions of their anger emerge nonetheless.

Depression

Depression is commonly referred to as anger turned inward. How many of your down moods or periods of depression are a direct result of you being angry at yourself for violating your own ethic? Most depression is rooted in unresolved anger, when you allow anger to simmer internally. You may allow it to simmer for so long that you have forgotten the original hurt that produced the anger. And now all you know is that you are depressed.

In our society, it is all too common to take a pill rather than identify the source and resolve it. Depression is like a fire alarm bell warning you that there is a potentially serious problem. But you don't like to hear the alarm bell, so you turn it off with a pill. Turning off the bell does not mean there is no problem. Now the small fire has the potential to become a five-alarm fire that is much more destructive and much more difficult to put out. As Plutarch, the second-century philosopher, said of the depressed person, "He looks on himself as a man whom the gods hate and pursue with their anger."

Emotional Coldness

Have you ever noticed how some people are emotionally cold? Is this you, from betraying yourself? Others are now afraid to touch you. You are like an iceberg. We see the visible part of the iceberg, but hidden underneath is a mass of coldness much greater than you or others can imagine.

The problem with anger is that humans cannot compartmentalize it. Once it starts, it grows like a cancer through the entire system if it is not identified and treated. The final result is you become an emotionally cold person who neither gives nor receives love and compassion.

Passive-Aggressive Behavior

Another disguised form of anger is passive–aggressive behavior. This is when you cannot be direct, open, honest, and appropriate about what you want. You cannot be open for fear of letting people know what is really inside you that you are hiding and harboring. Manipulators, who we have written about earlier, often display this behavior.

Saccharin-Sweet Behavior

Saccharin-sweet is a favorite phrase I use to describe self-anger. This is when you are so sweet that others find it difficult to have a deep relationship with you.

One who is saccharin-sweet is rarely thought to be an angry person. The problem is, one who uses this mechanism is no longer free to openly and clearly express how one feels. You have been hiding from self and others for so long now that you feel it is not safe to come out of your protective artificial sweetness.

And now you become so unhappy that you must find some way to ease your pain and loneliness, so you choose some method to distract your pain. It is common for folks with deep-seated anger to become addicted to food, drink, drugs, shopping, sex, or other addictive substances or behaviors.

The Inadequacy Monkey

When we live with guilt or anger at ourselves, we are not able to live up to our full potential. Anger has an effect on the brain; it actually impairs our ability to think. It is a physiological fact that the angrier we become, the more the blood drains from our brain and flows to our larger skeletal muscles. Thus, we become more physically competitive and more intellectually restricted. This leads us into some potentially serious actions resulting in terrible consequences. The frequent expression then is, "That was not me." Yes, it was you. Maybe not the normal day-to-day you, but it's the you who shows up when your anger—for which you are responsible—takes over. There is no such thing as, "He made me angry." You chose to become angry because he did something you did not like.

Jumping Monkeys

Have you ever watched a cage full of monkeys at the zoo? It's rare to find them sitting in one place. Instead, they seem to constantly jump around and trade places. Your psychological monkeys are similar:

- When your primary monkey is **fear**, it can jump and become anger or then guilt because of something you have done.

- When your primary monkey is **anger**, it can jump and become guilt.

- When your primary monkey is **guilt**, it can change and become the anger or inadequacy monkey or even manifest anxiety.

- When your primary monkey is **inadequacy**, it can become fear. Or anger because you want to defend yourself.

The principle is that you have one primary monkey, but your primary monkey can take on the attributes of another monkey for a period of time. However, your primary monkey is always present and directing your feelings and behavior.

An old man once said, "I have two dogs fighting in me all the time, a black dog and a white dog. The dog that I feed is the one that wins the battle of the day." You have four monkeys fighting to take control of your life. The one that you feed is the one that will control you today.

Points to Ponder

1. What core values did my family try to instill in me?

2. Have I ever betrayed myself? Have I done so once, a few times, or more often?

3. When I have betrayed myself, how has it affected me? What consequences have I experienced?

4. Which of the four psychological monkeys is the most powerful in my life?

5. What ideas do I have to help me develop a healthy balance in my life so I can stop betraying myself?

Chapter 8

When You Betray Others

Now for the really tough question. Whom have you rejected or betrayed?

In Chapter 3, we discussed the difference between rejection and betrayal. My experience is that all of us at some time have rejected someone and probably multiple people multiple times. The question is not, have you rejected someone—for we all have—but did you go beyond rejection and step into the shoes of betrayal? If so, what have you done to make it right with yourself and that person?

How did you react when you realized that you manipulated and betrayed another? Were you surprised? Disappointed? Did you keep going down the path, even when you recognized what you were doing? Your reaction to your act of betrayal is significant because it tells you—and others—what kind of person you really are.

Judas seemed to feel remorse because he took the thirty pieces of silver he had earned betraying Jesus and tried to return it to his co-conspirators. They didn't want it and so Judas

131

left it at their feet and went out and hanged himself. Was it guilt? Perhaps. Or was it disappointment that he did not get the result he wanted, which was probably for Jesus to overthrow the Roman government and place Judas in a place of leadership. We don't know.

Admit the Truth

If you betray someone, it is best to quickly admit it to yourself and then to the friend you have betrayed. You may lose the friendship, but think about what might happen if you don't confess. Likely, you will never again be a full and great friend and the friendship will die a sudden or slow death. To continue to try and hide your betrayal will put a serious strain on the relationship.

When husbands or wives betray one another, they can never get to a place of marital fulfillment while hiding the betrayal and hoping the other will not find out. I have many times dealt with couples who are struggling, and they do not know why. It is because one is holding a deep secret of betrayal, whether about money, an addiction, something sexual, or another matter. Yes, it is risky to get the truth out, but it is much better to do so. Sometimes it is best to make the confession with the assistance of a competent therapist. I don't recommend that you just blurt out your betrayal to your mate because soon you two will probably be in a major fight you may never recover from. I recommend that first you talk to a competent therapist or pastor and get their assistance in when and how to tell your mate or friend. Do not talk to a professional with an agenda of getting the professional on your side. Approach them with a genuine desire to get help solving this big issue. I recall reading one therapist who said the client often is thinking, "I come to you not to change or be changed, but to get you to agree with me and if I can get you to agree with me I can then convince anyone."

Notice the Patterns

In counseling we use a term called *patternicity*. This is when one demonstrates a pattern of consistent behavior, whether positive or negative. In other words, once we have done something a few times, we tend to easily repeat it. For example, you probably no longer even think about which shoe you put on first or how you tie your shoes. Since the day your parents taught you to tie your shoes, you just do it, and possibly just like they taught you. It usually takes considerable time and effort to break that habit, unless something dramatic happens such as breaking an arm, forcing you to find a new way to tie your shoes. Doing it a different way feels very clumsy.

Emotionally it is the same. Once you start down the road of betraying people, you will have a hard, but not impossible, time trying to change your behavior. Each time you reject, manipulate, or betray someone, you reinforce your behavior. The big problem is that your behavior may have gotten you what you wanted. So, you learned that this works.

As a therapist, my challenge is to help my clients see their pattern of belief or behavior, admit that they are doing it, and help them then work to change it, if they choose. This is difficult work. It is easy to say you want to change but once the process starts only the dedicated follow through. Many come to the counselor for help but sadly many drop out after just a few sessions.

It becomes even more difficult when one's environment reinforces one's established behavior. For example, if you want to stop drinking, you must stop going to the bar. That sounds easy enough, but now you are confronted with the loss of your friendships with the people who hang out there. So now you must not only stop drinking, but also stop where you go and whom you associate with. The possibility of change becomes less likely unless you work on building a new peer group.

We tend to behave in patterned ways whether the behavior is negative—like lying, cheating, or stealing—or positive—like opening a door for a person who has a disability. If you are accustomed to opening the door for a person with a disability, you will probably do so automatically, and even apologize to them if you're preoccupied and realize that you've failed to do it.

Make a Choice

Previously in this book I made reference to a client and it seems fitting to repeat it. I recall a client of mine who was referred to me by her company because she was known to be very manipulative. In our second session I addressed the issue directly. She began to sob dramatically; I sat quietly and waited for her to finish. When she stopped, I said, "I do not know if that is genuine remorse or if you are trying to manipulate me."

She said, "Neither do I."

To this day I do not know if she was showing genuine remorse, and she may never know either. After a couple more sessions, she quit the counseling. I suspect she just did not want to face herself and change.

The underlying question for both my client and for you is, are you unhappy enough with your behavior that you are ready to face yourself and your dysfunctional and destructive ways, or do you choose to continue as you are? The problem with continuing as you are is that you can't. There is no such thing as staying the same. You will either change and grow healthier, or you will continue to become more destructive to yourself and others.

Positive change is not easy, but it is worth it. Change is about you finding a more satisfying life and behavior for yourself and those around you. It is in your control; what do you want?

William Glasser, the founder of reality therapy, in his interesting chapter "Why It Makes Sense to Choose Misery" from his book *Take Effective Control of Your Life,* says, "You probably find it difficult to believe that you not only choose most of the misery you suffer, but that choosing misery almost always makes sense at the time."[1]

Even in choosing misery we are attempting to take control of our lives. However, being in total control of our lives is an illusion.

Again, Glasser, in his book *Reality Therapy,* says the three Rs of reality therapy are Reality, Responsibility, and Right and Wrong.[2] To change, we must be willing to accept these fundamental concepts and commit ourselves to them. He says, "Once we become involved with a patient and teach him new ways of behavior, his attitude will change regardless of whether or not he understands his old ways, and then his new attitude will promote further behavioral change."[3]

"Our job is to confront them with their total behavior, and then get them to judge the quality of what they are doing. We have found that unless they judge their own behavior, they will not change."[4]

Many people are inclined to use negative or destructive ways to get their needs of "relatedness and respect" met.[5]

Psychiatrists and psychologists frequently write about the importance of getting our needs met. Different authors use different words such as *love, respect, appreciation*, and *relatedness*; however, they all have the same goal.

Peggy Papp, an internationally known psychotherapist says, "Since change and stability are viewed as two sides of the same coin, the choice is purely a pragmatic one. All change can be understood as the effort to maintain some constancy, and all constancy is maintained through change."[6]

The bottom line is, you are in control of your life. Will you choose contentment and happy relationships or misery and broken relationships?

There is no such thing as not choosing. By not choosing you are choosing not to change.

Forgive Yourself

Once you've admitted to the betrayal and made the choice to change, take the necessary step of forgiving yourself. Janis Abrahms Spring, in her book *How Can I Forgive You?*, says, "Self-forgiveness is not something you do just to make yourself feel better. It is something you do to make yourself *be* better."[7]

How to change and move forward are discussed in detail in Chapter 13.

Points to Ponder

1. Am I ready to forgive myself?

2. Have I asked the friend I betrayed for forgiveness?

3. What am I getting out of my suffering?

Chapter 9

Betrayal by the Church

My experience is that most of us hold one of three opinions about church and other religious institutions. You either believe in the concept and support it, you dislike it and hold some strong feelings against it, or you are indifferent.

I know many who are grateful and happy with how the church has contributed in a positive way to their life and to their family's lives. Most have no illusion that all people in any church are perfect. Typically, these people are realists who are well aware of their own and humanity's frailty.

Yet over the years I have heard some who are very angry at the church. They say, "The church betrayed me." While it may be likely that they feel they were mistreated in some way, it is a bit of overstatement to declare the whole church or religious institution failed them.

My grandmother, my father's mother, was a fine lady of faith who lived her faith but never pushed it on others. I am told that she raised my father in the church. One day, while he was married to my mother, he heard the minister say something he did not like, and he vowed he would never go to church again. And he never did. Almost never. The only time I saw him in church was when the church building was on fire and he—being a fireman—went in. I recall seeing him run out as the roof fell in.

Clearly my father's life and commitment to his wife and children went downhill once he left the church. I will never know if he used his unhappiness with whatever it was that the minister said as an excuse to leave the church because he was already on the silent downward slide, or if he just used what the minister said to justify his abandonment of his values.

It's the Person, Not the Institution

In truth, *no* church or religious institution can betray you. A church is an institution, not a person. A church comprises many diverse people; it is most likely that only one person—or a few at most—betrayed you, abused you, lied to you, neglected you, or spread gossip.

Unfortunately, these occurrences are all too common. I am not making excuses; I am merely stating a fact that every institution has its share of incompetent, insensitive, and unloving people. We tend to see the people with negative traits first, forgetting that churches and religious institutions also have many caring and loving people.

We also lose sight of the fact that when we are part of an institution, we too can easily display these same negative traits. We are capable of them all and we are not perfect *either*. We are never justified in hurting others, but, sadly, we do so anyway, whether we are part of a religious group or not.

When we have a "bad experience" with a church, we tend to condemn all religious people and institutions. When you think only bad things come from churches or religious organizations, I encourage you to do some research on the people and religious institutions that have made positive contributions to America and to the world, including the individuals who founded America and those who wrote our wonderful Constitution with the concepts of freedom that we now enjoy. Did you know that many of the major universities (e.g., Yale, Harvard, Princeton) were founded by religious people? Many hospitals were founded by religious institutions and some are still run by the Catholic Church as well as denominations such as Baptists, Methodists and others .

I find it interesting that when a person has been betrayed by someone in a church, the betrayed one often condemns the church as a whole and vows never to have anything to do with one again. Yet when a friend is the betrayer, the person betrayed rarely stops engaging in all friendships. And when a family member is the betrayer, the person doesn't *typically* reject every member of the family, or the concept of *family* altogether.

Families, friends, churches, and governments are full of flawed people, including you and me, and all of us do hurtful things to other people. Even so, being rejected and betrayed ourselves doesn't give us license to reject or betray others.

It is a fact that there are hypocrites in every church. Friend, the fact is we are all hypocrites to some degree because none of us always measures up to what we believe or profess. The world is full of people; therefore, it is also full of hypocrites.

The word *hypocrite* comes from the Greek word *hypokritēs*, which means "stage actor"—one who pretends to be what he is not. In Greek plays, the actors would hold up different masks when they were playing different roles. Thus, a play could be performed with fewer actors and less need for frequent costume changes. Let's face it: psychologists and psychiatrists are the first to acknowledge that we have multiple sides to our personalities. That does not mean we are clinically multiple personalities. We all have some different masks we wear in different situations. Isn't it fun to put some formal clothing or a costume on a young person and watch them take on a different behavior?

I have a real problem with this concept of hypocrite. I think it is true that each of us at times—and some more than others—are not what we present ourselves to be. But I don't think hurtful hypocrisy is as common as many think. And I've found that even hypocrites tend to have more positive traits than negative.

When I was a chaplain in a maximum-security prison, I engaged with many who had done some very bad things. It is true that their illegal behavior was very destructive to others. As I got to know them, however, I also saw their positive sides. Though some were thieves, they did not steal all day every day. Though some were murderers, they did not kill all day every day. Much of the inmates' day was as normal as yours. This is not for one moment intended to justify hurtful or destructive behavior to our fellow life journeyer. Or excuse criminal behavior.

We are all human with human frailties. This is not to suggest that we should either reject everyone or approve of poor manners and mean-spiritedness. Find the middle ground and treat others like you want to be treated. It is okay to keep in mind what they did, so you can stay alert to the next time, if there is one. Remembering and being alert is not the same as hating.

As a young child our family always had dogs; I was and am a dog lover. I would often go next door to play with the neighbors' dog, which was chained. I did so with my neighbors' permission. One day, their dog suddenly lunged at me and bit right through my lip. I had to go through a series of pre-rabies shots. To this day I still love dogs. I do not hate or fear all dogs because of what happened to me when I was a child.

Our relationship with the church is not unlike our relationship with our family and friends. We start out trusting them, because most relationships start with some level of trust. Over time, a person may disappoint us and then all we can see is that one black spot, looming large. We lose perspective on all the good they have done us and others. We do turn against the person or persons, because we are protecting ourselves and do not want to get hurt again.

Perhaps you've seen the old routine of putting a small black spot on a white sheet of paper and being asked what you see. Interestingly, even if you are aware of the "trick," your eyes and your mind still gravitate toward the black spot. We tend to first only see the negative, rather than the much larger, spotless area around the dot.

May I suggest an alternative. When you have been deceived, rejected, or betrayed, accept the fact that it was one person who did it, or possibly a few, but it probably was not everyone in that group. Nor was it the whole world.

Yes, some in the group were weak, or possibly did not know what was going on, and did not stand up for you. However, do not automatically reject everyone in a group because of the behavior of a few. If you follow that pattern, you will soon find yourself all alone in a small room. Being alone is not painless, nor is it an escape from hurt. Loneliness is extremely painful; it even drives some people to take their own life or the life of another.

Jordan Peterson, in his great book *12 Rules for Life: An Antidote to Chaos,* very directly says we should accept that "life doesn't have the problem. You do."[1]

Ouch, that hurts because we are good at blaming others to excuse our own thoughts and behaviors.

Why do we blame others? The biggest reason is that we place our expectations on others. When they do not fulfill our preconceived expectations, we get upset or disappointed and sometimes even feel we have been betrayed when in fact we have not been betrayed or rejected. Worst of all, they did not even know we had those expectations of them.

The great psychiatrist Sigmund Freud, many years ago, identified several ego defense mechanisms. Ego defense mechanisms are psychological strategies that are unconsciously used to protect a person from anxiety arising from unacceptable thoughts or feelings.

I believe that projection is one of the most commonly used ego defense mechanisms in our society. Projection is when you put your feelings or thoughts onto another person, as though they were that person's feelings and thoughts. This is something we do unconsciously to reduce our own fear, anxiety, or insecurity. If it were being consciously done, we would probably be very unhappy with ourselves. Putting it simply, we accuse others of things that we think about, are doing or are going to do, but do not want to admit to ourselves.

Spiritual but not Religious

Some of you may say you are spiritual but not religious. The majority of the great leading psychologists and psychiatrists agree that all humans have a spiritual core. One may or may not express their spirituality through a religious affiliation or practice. But it is the spiritual core that separates the human from all other creatures. Viktor Frankl, the famed Austrian psychiatrist and Auschwitz survivor, studied himself and his fellow man in the midst of their struggle for survival. In *The Unconscious God,* he wrote about man's spiritual core and need for meaning through being religious. He wrote:

> On his way to find the ultimate meaning of life, the irreligious man, as it were, has not yet reached the highest peak, but rather has stopped at the next to highest .... And what is the reason the irreligious man does not go further? It is because he does not want to lose the "firm ground under his feet." The true summit is barred from his vision; it is hidden, in the fog, and he does not risk venturing into it, into this uncertainty. Only the religious man hazards it.[2]

Further on he writes:

> Clinical evidence suggests that atrophy of the religious sense results in a distortion of his religious concepts. Or, to put it in a less clinical vein, once the angel in us is repressed, he turns into a demon.[3]

What about God?

We find it much easier to reject a religious institution than God or the Bible. Again, like the church we all have an opinion. You either believe in God or you don't, or you have not taken a serious look, so you have no opinion.

Now I will let a highly regarded scholar challenge your view of God and the Bible. After you read this, I will reveal the author, as I do not want to prejudice your reading before you read the quotes.

Does that mean that what we see is dependent on our religious beliefs? Yes! And what we don't see, as well! You might object, "But I'm an atheist." No, you're not (and if you want to understand this, you could read Dostoevsky's *Crime and Punishment,* perhaps the greatest novel ever written, in which the main character, Raskolnikov, decides to take his atheism with true seriousness, commits what he has rationalized as a benevolent murder, and pays the price). You're simply not an atheist in your actions, and it is your actions that most accurately reflect your deepest beliefs—those that are implicit, embedded in your being, underneath your conscious apprehensions and articulable attitudes and surface-level self-knowledge. You can only find out what you actually believe (rather than what you think you believe) by watching how you act. You simply don't know what you believe, before that. You are too complex to understand yourself.[4]

The Bible is, for better or worse, the foundational document of Western civilization (of Western values, Western morality, and Western conceptions of good and evil).... The Bible is a library composed of many books, each written and edited by many people. It's a truly emergent document—a selected, sequenced and finally coherent story written by no one and everyone over many thousands of years. The Bible has been thrown up, out of the deep, by the collective human imagination, which is itself a product of unimaginable forces operating over unfathomable spans of time. Its careful, respectful study can reveal things to us about what we believe and how we do and should act that can be discovered in almost no other manner.[5]

These quotes are from Jordan Peterson's *12 Rules for Life: An Antidote to Chaos.* Surprising, since the author is not a theologian or a pastor. Peterson is a clinical psychologist at the highly respected University of Toronto. Google him and see his full bio.

I hope I have stirred things up in you that you will take some time to consider, whatever your position on God or the church. It's important to not just hold to what you have been defending. It is also good to take a long look at oneself and reevaluate.

If, when all your life is going well, you can easily say you are an atheist or agnostic, what are you going to do when life comes crashing down on you? When your small child whom you love is gravely ill and could die at any moment? When you are desperately ill and possibly on your death bed? When your family has deserted you and you are all alone in an empty house? When you are in the middle of a life crisis and have lost everything? Remember the old World War II statement, "There are no atheists in foxholes."

In my experience, I've seen many atheists and agnostics seek prayer in times of severe distress. On one Sunday morning, an unknown man came rushing into a church I was attending, desperately wanting to talk to someone. He asked for advice and prayer for his two newborn, seriously deformed sons. I listened to him and encouraged him, and we agreed to meet again later that day. He did not show for our meeting, and he would not return my calls. When I finally did reach him, he told me that the babies had died, and he no longer wanted any contact with the church or with me. The crisis is over—I do not need God now!

When people in these crisis situations—who have had no interest in spiritual things or God prior to the event—do not get the immediate answer they want, they wonder why God did not answer their desperate prayers the way they wanted him to, when they wanted him to. And now they are angry at God.

One more thought. If you declare yourself to be an atheist, you are stating that there is no God. In order to be definitive in your belief, then you must be all-knowing. And I doubt you are all-knowing about anything.

Truthfully, what you are saying is, "I do not believe," and that is different from declaring there is no God. It is easy for me to remember Madalyn Murray O'Hair declaring "God is dead" and leading a movement in the early 1960s to take prayer out of the schools. I bet you forgot all about her, or you've never heard of her. Of course, she could not prove her position. What I do know is that today she is dead. And would you say we have a better world now because of her crusade? It's most interesting that her son, William J. Murray, is a Baptist minister and lobbyist. He now lobbies Congress to restore religious rights, trying to undo what his mother did.

If you have been betrayed or mistreated by a church or religious organization, take some time to reflect on why you hold your position. For your own best interest, do not carry a grudge or hatred.

I encourage you to apply the same techniques I recommend in Chapters 12 and 13 to grow beyond your feeling of being betrayed by the church. And if you like or want to challenge Jordan Peterson, I recommend you get his book and read it all.

Points to Ponder

1. Do I really know why I hold to my position on church and on God?

2. Am I a better person for not holding to any religious beliefs?

3. Are my expectations of God selfish and unrealistic?

Chapter 10

Betrayal by the Community

There are four areas that consume much of our lives and bring us the most joy or pain: our family, our friends, the church, and the community. We have already addressed betrayal by family, friends, and the church; now it is time to take a look at the community—specifically the workplace and government.

We cannot escape any of these unless we decide to live alone in some remote place. And granted, sometimes we all want to escape to such a place to get away from all the rejection, betrayal, and pain in our lives. But once we finish daydreaming, we come back to reality and decide to work through the challenge. The real challenge for us is to work through our betrayal in positive ways and not carry bitterness. Bitterness is always self-destructive.

The most common factor of betrayal within the workplace and government is that both rarely measure up to our expectations. At best, each partially meets our expectations. Sometimes employers help set our expectations in order to win us over. For example, when we are hired into a new position, our new employer makes all kinds of promises so we'll accept their offer. The same is true for government; politicians make a lot of promises to get our vote.

Frequently, people ask, "Is it the system's fault or an individual's fault that promises and expectations are not fulfilled?" I have heard that discussion many times and my answer is always, "It's people."

Systems are just systems; they are not human. They cannot make or keep promises. Humans make and operate systems. I get tired of excuses like, "There is a problem with our computer system." Not so. Someone made the system or programmed the system incorrectly. It did not make itself. It is probably true that you do not have a clue as to who made the software or electronics, but someone made it. And some workers are more skilled than others. For example, all doctors passed their boards, but all are not equal in their ability. A humorous, but factual way to look at is fifty percent of all doctors graduated at the bottom have of their class.

Business and government are systems that are designed and operated by humans. And yes, there are often tragic flaws in both that cause many to suffer. Our problem is that we want to trust both because we want to have order and not chaos or uncertainty in our lives. We have a very difficult time living in a total state of uncertainty or anxiety, so we trust. Trust is essential to an orderly life and society. As trust erodes, anxiety increases.

Unfortunately, sometimes our trust in a system is broken. When our trust is broken, we experience a loss of small or great proportions and we must deal with the loss and the anxiety it brings. We'll talk more about this in Chapter 12, "Overcoming the Pain."

Expectations

We have three types of expectations:

- Ours and theirs
- Our valid expectations
- Our unrealistic expectations

When our trust has been broken, we really need to sort out whether our expectations were valid or whether they were unrealistic. Yes, there are times when the people who operate a business or the government completely and consciously violate our trust. And there are times when we have been living with unrealistic expectations.

Betrayal in the Workplace

We are still holding on to the myth of lifetime employment by one employer. Actually, this only existed for about forty years in the history of work in America—from just after the WW II to about the 1980s, at most. My grandfather was one who retired with a gold watch and a pension.

Prior to the WWII, a very high percentage of workers were self-employed as farmers or shop keepers, or were engaged in small home industries or trades such as that of a blacksmith, buggy maker, or something similar. The term *journeyman* is still used today to refer to someone training in a trade and working for someone on a per-day basis. Originally it meant someone with a bag of tools who traveled from town to town looking for work.

When I assist people with their career planning, I always try to help them to see that they are in charge of their career, not their employer. I tell them, "When you are employed, be sure to be a faithful, loyal employee. Simultaneously, pay attention to what is happening to your career."

When I worked in the outplacement industry, my job was to be onsite when someone's job was being terminated and to help the displaced worker with their career and life transition. It never ceased to amaze me at how completely shocked most people were, even when they knew the business was not going well. Shock leads to anger, which leads to blaming the company.

Let me say it again: be in charge of your own career and finances and then you will not blame the company.

When you feel your workplace has betrayed you, ask yourself these questions:

- Do I really believe that my employer can always, in every circumstance, fulfill every one of their commitments?

- Do I really believe that the company's first concern is my welfare? Sorry, but that is an invalid expectation because the company has a fiduciary responsibility to its investors, not to its employees. And there are many circumstances beyond your employer's control that affect them and you, such as a major downturn in the economy. For many years, a myth has propagated that the company will take care of you once you are employed. Note that I said *myth*. Myths are when many people believe something that usually is not true in order to keep their anxiety down. Even though everyone knows the truth, no one addresses it publicly. It is like the old saying there is an elephant in the room, but no one comments. Or the famous fable of the emperor's clothes. Remember how he believed he had on the most beautiful clothes and walked down the street naked? It took a child to point out the emperor did not have any clothes on.

It's important to restate that without trust, our lives would be unbearable. So, we choose to trust the employer, our government, our friends or family until they violate that trust. Daily now, we see that companies are laying off workers and closing businesses. This is not a trend; this pattern will continue as companies and products become obsolete. Have you seen any recent demand for buggy whips, dial-up modems, or Polaroid cameras?

I recall one gentleman who came to our outplacement office faithfully every day for months. He was working hard to find a new position. One day we got a call from his wife who had heard from a friend that he was at our office. He had never told his wife that he had been terminated and was busy looking for a new position. He was too embarrassed to tell her.

To live an orderly life, we must trust our spouses, family, friends, church, workplaces, and government. Because we live with trust and hope, we just do not want to see problems even though they are evident. It is called *denial*. Denial is part of our humanness. On the other hand, we must also remain vigilant. Balancing trust and vigilance is not always easy.

As one who has considerable experience consulting to the business world, I am well aware that most everyone will experience disappointment at some point in their work career. Many people may experience disappointment multiple times.

There is nothing wrong with the idea of a "self-driving" car, but it did not make and program itself. Self-driving is a misnomer. Someone programmed it and is driving you. You just cannot see them. I won't be buying one anytime in the near future because I expect there to be many accidents in the technology's early days. I do not completely trust even the brightest humans to think of all the issues and fix them. Humans can't think of everything and they frequently make poor decisions. We are still hearing about the Boeing 737 MAX planes, which were grounded after two tragic crashes.

I recall being asked to evaluate a pilot who had recently crashed the corporate jet. The corporation contended it was pilot error and the pilot contended it was jet malfunction. I interviewed the pilot and administered a number of personality and concentration tests. When he came back a few days later for the results, I told him I would never fly with him because I could see his problems from the tests. He then admitted, "I always knew I wasn't a good pilot." Yes, there was a small engine malfunction but not one significant enough to cause the plane to crash. The pilot had lost his concentration and crashed the plane.

You are responsible for your life and career. Just like you are responsible for the car you are driving.

In Government

I am very grateful that I was born in the United States of America. And I am a staunch defender of our Constitution and way of government. But I also know that America is not perfect nor is the government run by perfect people. Everyone has their own view and beliefs. In my view, problems occur when a citizen's or politician's beliefs or opinions are radically different from those in the Constitution or Bill of Rights. Or there are biased decisions that injure or destroy others.

Or a leader fails in a big way to expeditiously execute their responsibilities.

One of the more recent tragedies that is still festering is the Benghazi disaster, the failure to act to protect and rescue courageous diplomats and soldiers. In my opinion, lies were propagated to protect the government officials in charge.

Sometimes biases, incompetence, or personal agendas can result in serious accusations and convictions of innocent men and women. This is usually not the fault of the rules established by government, but by human failings. I am not excusing anyone's behavior, but I am trying to stress that we are all very flawed people.

Based on my experience of working in the prison system and as a therapist, as well as the experience of my social circle, I know of folks who were overly prosecuted because a federal agent, prosecutor, or judge was determined to punish someone they did not like. Sometimes someone is persecuted for years, far beyond what is technically legal. The problem here is not government, but an angry, biased person. I have a personal friend who received considerable injustice.

Unfortunately—or fortunately—government is not a machine (and if it were, it would still sometimes fail).

The reality of life is that we are going to be disappointed or feel betrayed by politicians who say one thing and do another. In defense of politicians, there are some good ones and we need them. We need people who will work to help us have an orderly government. And in all fairness to them, your politician may be working for you, but they are only one person among many.

The real challenge we have is managing ourselves in good times and bad because we cannot control all the systems and people around us.

Then again there are those who profess allegiance to the country and their position, yet they have a secret goal and motive to undo or destroy the country's foundation. They are betrayers.

We must not forget the horrible impact of war on a country and all families. Some families are more tragically impacted than others. But in wartime, everyone suffers in some way—some greater, some lesser. This is not the place to discuss anyone's political positions on war. However, I do want to discuss the impact of war on citizens.

During World War II, many children in England were put on trains and sent into the countryside for safekeeping from the bombing. They were given to families at random, usually farm families, and put to work. While the intention of their parents and government may have been noble to protect them from the bombing, many were seriously emotionally damaged and saw what happened to them as abandonment and betrayal. They carried lifetime scars.

We probably agree that terrible things may have happened to you and your family. This is never acceptable. Even when someone did a dastardly deed, we must do our best to overcome it and forgive them. No matter how bad the deed was, in order for us to maintain our own mental health, we must apply the correct principles of good mental health for ourselves and our families.

Read on to Chapter 12, "Overcoming the Pain," and Chapter 13, "Growing Beyond Betrayal." I want to give you hope and a pathway to good mental health.

To quote Mother Teresa, "I used to believe that prayer changes things, but now I know that prayer changes us, and we change things."

Points to Ponder

1. What unrealistic expectations do I have of my employer or government?

2. How can I balance trusting while simultaneously being aware of the risk?

3. Am I holding on to my disappointment or betrayal, or have I moved on?

Chapter 11

Your Reaction to Betrayal

How you react to a betrayal is completely personal. I have seen a lot of clients and friends hit by betrayal and I can never predict how a person is going to respond. The variables are so many that it is impossible to predict your own or another's response.

One's response can be anything from a mild to a severe reaction. Some people become dangerous to themselves and to others or the betrayer. The reaction can be immediate, or it could erupt unpredictably, at any time. We have all heard and seen many tragic stories in the media of persons who went into a school, workplace, or other public venue and suddenly killed many people. Many of them had a simmering rage that they had nursed for a long time because they believed they had been betrayed by a boss, coworker, friend, family member, or even society. I certainly saw far too many of these people when I worked in the prison system.

At times we see riots with looting, destruction, and even physical abuse of others. The people committing these violent acts use any opportunity to act out their pent-up rage—anger they have been repressing for a long time. Much of their rage has little to do with whatever the present political climate is. They just use the present situation as an excuse to act out their rage.

The point is, it is not what happened to you or by whom. **It is about how *you* see it.** Are you strong enough to handle it or are you so fragile that you are not able to take the blow? How strong or weak are your self-esteem and self-control? How many previous betrayals and rejections have you endured?

As observers, we do not know the answers to the above questions. Nor do the best therapists ever fully know what is in the deep recesses of another's mind and emotions. Often, the individual is not even aware of the degree of their own hostility and anger and its potential for destruction.

It seems that the more one was dependent on the betrayer, the more difficult it is for one to quickly accept what is happening and react in a healthy way. The more one is independent of the betrayer, the easier it is for one to adapt because they have not lost their whole world.

Also important is having a strong support network of family and friends. This is often the crucial factor in how one handles the crisis. Loners have no one to talk it out with.

There is always the potential for many responses both healthy and less healthy. Hopefully you will pick the healthy strategies even if you struggle a bit with the less healthy ones.

Healthy Coping Techniques

Acceptance, forgiveness, and taking care of yourself are three ways to handle the immediate shock of betrayal. We will talk about each of these in more detail below.

Acceptance

Acceptance is both the first stage and the last stage of the grieving process. The first phase of acceptance is not full acceptance; it is just the beginning of facing reality. You must begin the grieving process, so you can move to fully accept what has happened. You need to begin to process the betrayal and face the emotional responses, which are inevitable.

When I was in graduate school, my professor, a student of Dr. Elizabeth Kübler-Ross, in our class on death and dying, shared directly with us Ross's research on the five stages of grief when one is dying. Since then her research has become commonly accepted and some use the stages to describe any loss. The stages are denial, bargaining, anger, depression, and finally acceptance. Our challenge is to move through the stages in a reasonable period of time without getting stuck in any one stage.

When the betrayal is very serious, like the destruction of a marriage, it may take up to eighteen months to get to full acceptance. Someone who says after a few short weeks, "I am over it and into acceptance," may actually still be in the denial stage. This is false acceptance. They are deceiving themselves because in some ways they want to quickly get past the pain, forget what happened, and move on. However, they are still actually conflicted in the denial stage.

The denial stage helps us avoid facing the full impact of the loss at one time and lets the pain and reality in slowly. At a deeper level, we fear what is coming in the form of life-changing circumstances, shame, and loneliness. When a marriage is destroyed, it is very dangerous to immediately go out and get into a new relationship. (Did you know that second marriages have a higher divorce rate than first marriages?)

When someone has betrayed us, we grieve much like we do when a friend or mate has died because there is a significant loss. If trust is severely wounded or completely eliminated, sometimes the relationship is totally destroyed. Part of our way of life dies and one must begin to build a new life. You cannot rebuild your life, because that cannot happen. You cannot go back to where you were at any time in the past. The past is past. The present is here.

Forgiveness

Forgiveness is always essential to being able to move on with your life in a healthy way. We'll talk about forgiveness in detail in Chapter 13, "Growing Beyond Betrayal."

Self-Care

Now is the time you need to take extra care of yourself physically, emotionally, and spiritually. Enjoy your friends. Make new ones. Take care of yourself by taking the risk to forgive graciously.

Henri Nouwen, in his outstanding book, *The Return of the Prodigal Son: A Homecoming,* wrote:

> Both trust and gratitude require the courage to take risks because distrust and resentment, in their need to keep their claim on me, keep warning me how dangerous it is to let go of my careful calculations and guarded predictions. At many points I have to make a leap of faith to let trust and gratitude have a chance to write a gentle letter to someone who will not forgive me, make a call to

someone who has rejected me, speak a word of healing to someone who cannot do the same. The leap of faith always means loving without expecting to be loved in return.[1]

Unhealthy Coping Techniques

Not every coping technique is healthy. Getting stuck in anger, seeking revenge, going into withdrawal, shutting down emotionally, or turning to addictive substances are all ways of coping, but ultimately will not help you move beyond the betrayal.

Anger

It's not uncommon to be angry about the betrayal. We talked about this in previous chapters. Getting in stuck in anger, however, can lead you to abuse others or yourself. You may even sink into a deep depression.

Revenge

Revenge is one way of acting out your anger. The problem with revenge is that it never satisfies us and always leaves us in a worse state than before the betrayal. We may think we are getting even or punishing our betrayer; however, we end up destroying ourselves.

Remember what we stated earlier: if you think your betrayer has the same level of guilt you would have, you are going to be very disappointed. If you keep trying to get them to accept what they did to you and apologize, to use an old expression, you are beating your head against the wall. Or as the old adage goes, "He who throws dirt, loses ground."

Can you tell me of one person who took revenge and did not suffer more? I urge you to stay out of the revenge business. Do you enjoy the company of angry, vengeful people? I doubt it. I don't. And your friends will not like you to be that way either and will soon abandon you.

The betrayer will sooner or later get their punishment. My father, whether he recognized it or not, lost not only his wife, but also the joy of participating in his children's and grandchildren's lives. He died a lonely man with cirrhosis, with only one person in his life. He thought he had friends, but my observation is that they tolerated him. Isn't that punishment enough?

If you really want to get revenge, take great care of yourself. Enjoy new friends and activities. Let your betrayer or rejecter see that you have a great life without them. This will hurt them more than anything you can do.

Withdrawal

Withdrawing from others because you feel shame is not healthy. You need to remember that you are not responsible for the other person's behavior, and you should be rejoicing that you have found out who they really are before they hurt you even more.

This is the time to reach out to your good friends and spend time with them. Do not turn them down when they reach out to you. If you do that too frequently, they may go away, and you will be more alone.

If, on the other hand, you are reaching out to someone who is hurting and they are pushing you away, they may be hiding. When I have been asked by someone who is trying to reach out to a hurting friend and they are being rejected, I tell them that I firmly believe that their friend does not want them to go away; they are just overcome with embarrassment, shame, sadness, and depression. I believe they are actually saying, "Go away and come closer." They don't feel good enough about themselves to receive you and your kindness.

Emotional Shutdown

Emotional shutdown is similar to withdrawal. Here, the difference is that you shut down your emotional being, and you soon become a cold, unemotional person.

Think of someone you know who is shut down for any reason and ask yourself if you think they are living a joyful life. Do you really want to become like this? It can happen suddenly or over a period of time. Their gravestone will read, "Died at 40, buried at 80." What do you want yours to say? How about, "She overcame victoriously."

Addiction

Surrendering your life to addiction to drugs, alcohol, food, or whatever, is a slow death you are imposing on yourself, physically and emotionally. *Again, remember that addiction does not hurt your betrayer, it hurts you.* (Yes, throughout this little book, we have repeated this truth many times.) In fact, as they see you depressed or down and out, more likely they will not be moved with compassion. Instead they will be glad they abandoned you, because they will see you as a weak person. They probably already despise weak people.

No, now is the time for you to start a new life—one that will be better than the one you had before you were betrayed.

Points to Ponder

1. Where am I in the cycle of anger, denial, bargaining, depression, and acceptance?

2. What healthy coping mechanisms, if any, am I using to manage myself after the betrayal?

3. What unhealthy coping mechanisms, if any, am I using to manage myself after the betrayal?

Chapter 12

Overcoming the Pain

"Despair is suffering without meaning."

This was written by Viktor Frankl, the renowned Austrian psychiatrist who suffered with many others as a Jewish prisoner at Auschwitz and Dachau concentration camps. Over one million Jews died in the camps, some by extermination and others by abuse and deprivation; others just gave up and died.

As both psychiatrist and prisoner, Frankl was in a unique— but not desired—position to view man's struggle to survive in a brutal, deadly environment. I cannot envision a more horrible place of abuse and suffering, with captives not knowing when or if they would be sent to the extermination furnaces.

Upon exiting the prison, Frankl wrote two classics, *Man's Search for Meaning* and *The Unconscious God,* about his observation of brutality and survival. When you are struggling with betrayal and despair, I strongly urge you to read them, especially *Man's Search for Meaning.* I know you are not in a worse situation than he and fellow prisoners faced.

Frankl's core theme is that in order to survive suffering, one must find some purpose or meaning to life beyond the present suffering. While in the camps, he noticed that some of his fellow prisoners vowed they would survive so they could get even with a brutal guard. Others wanted to stay alive to see their family and others who were important to them.

Frankl noted that it did not matter what each individual saw as their meaning; what mattered was that they unwaveringly held to their meaning and their purpose for survival. When Frankl saw someone wavering or giving up on their purpose for surviving, he knew they would soon die if he could not help them regain their sense of meaning and purpose. Sometimes he was successful; unfortunately, sometimes he was not.

Below are some quotes from *Man's Search for Meaning*. I've found these to be extremely helpful for my clients to consider when they are experiencing despair.

We had to learn ourselves and, furthermore, we had to teach the despairing men, that *it did not really matter what we expected from life, but rather what life expected from us.*[1]

Suffering is an inevitable part of life, even as fate and death. Without suffering and death human life cannot be complete.[2]

Man can preserve a vestige of spiritual freedom, of independence of mind, even in such terrible conditions of psychic and physical stress.[3]

Fundamentally, therefore, any man can, even under such circumstances, decide what shall become of him—mentally and spiritually. He may retain his human dignity even in a concentration camp. Dostoevsky said once, "There is only one thing I dread: not to be worthy of my sufferings."[4]

In *Man's Search for Meaning*, Frankl appears to be a great fan of the philosopher Nietzsche. He references him often.

That which does not kill me, makes me stronger.[5]

As we said before, any attempt to restore a man's inner strength in the camp had first to succeed in showing him some future goal. Nietzsche's words, "He who has a *why* to live for can bear with almost any *how*."[6]

The problem is we often do not get to the *why* and we are left wondering or blaming ourselves or others. We must decide to move beyond this.

Clearly Frankl and others in the prison had been betrayed by their governments and fellow citizens to end up in such a horrible situation. However, they were not the only persons to experience betrayal and extreme suffering.

Many people have been betrayed and suffered greatly because of others' corrupt or calloused hearts. As Frankl teaches us, no matter the circumstances, we too get to choose how we will see the situation, the betrayer, and ourselves. No one put it more concisely than motivational guru Dale Carnegie when he quoted his father:

Two men looked out from prison bars,
One saw the mud, the other saw the stars.[7]

I agree with Carnegie. When I worked in a maximum-security prison, I saw many who tried to fight the system and others. They only ended up making themselves miserable and limiting more of their freedoms. Those who accepted that they were responsible for their situation adapted and were less angry and frustrated.

Resolving Past Betrayals

"Growing Beyond Betrayal" is the subtitle of this book because overcoming the deep emotional wound of betrayal is a major battle which you can grow beyond and come out a much better person. It is challenging to regain one's emotional equilibrium and come to full healing, but it can be done and many before you have come through it successfully.

All victims of betrayal are truly victims because no one deserves to be betrayed. Betrayal is an extremely deep violation of a relationship because it is the breaking and crushing of trust. Nothing is more important or fragile in a relationship than trust. Breaking it is a moral wounding. Some wounds are much deeper and more destructive than others. However, all betrayal is a serious wounding of one's inner core.

How are you going to handle and overcome your betrayal? How are you going to *choose*—notice I say choose—to spend your life? Are you going to play victim, seek revenge, and become bitter and unlovable? Or are you going to deal with the pain and move on?

You did not have control over who deceived you or how you were deceived, rejected, or betrayed. You do have control over how you are going to respond and live.

I would like to challenge you to look at your experience of the Judas Kiss and recognize that although it was a very painful and hurtful time, you need to look up and acknowledge that it could have been much worse. As a therapist, I often helped people through the Judas Kiss and as they came out from the pain, they too realized that life was better now than it had been with the Judas in their life. They were now free of the underlying fear, suspicion, and doubt that so often accompanies life with a betrayer before a betrayer reveals themselves for who they are. They were now free of constantly wondering what is wrong with them that they could never win over the genuine love of this person. By now in this book I hope you understand who your betrayer is, and that you never could win their love and respect because they are incapable of giving it.

Now that you know the truth and are working through the pain, and after years of deep uncertainty, you are going to be freer than you could have ever expected. There is an old statement that is so true, "You will know the truth, and the truth will set you free." However, first it will make you miserable as you work through the pain from your betrayer.

What I did not know as an adolescent was that, as an adult, I would experience two additional painful family betrayals. Resolving the first one helped me get through the next two. Although I still experienced a lot of pain, I did not develop any residual destructive anger.

I recommend that you resolve each betrayal as it comes, so that you can get through any subsequent betrayals with a healthier mind and soul. It is like any other activity: the more you learn how to do it, the easier the next time will be.

It has been my privilege of working with many clients who had to deal with betrayal in one form or another. Those who had unresolved bitterness from the past had a much harder time getting through the present situation. Unresolved bitterness from the past compounds the pain in the present and makes the present betrayal even more painful. Whenever

I see someone with much more pain and anger than would normally be typical for the situation, I immediately suspect unresolved historical pain. Our job is much more difficult because now we must work on both the present and the past at the same time.

Two Causes of Betrayal Pain

There are at least two primary causes as to why being betrayed is so painful.

First Primary Hurt

The first primary hurt is broken trust, as we have mentioned previously. Trust is an essential human trait. It is unique to human beings and is never experienced by animals. It is innate in us and we cannot live without it. It is as important to life as the air we breathe, more precious and fragile than any porcelain vase.

Trust often takes a long time to build but can be crushed in a moment and is not easy to restore. Trust should not be taken lightly. It should not be taken for granted as though it is deserved. No, it needs to be earned.

Remember Humpty Dumpty? All the king's horses and all the king's men could not put him together again. And often the best therapist cannot help their client to restore their core of trust that was broken, because the client has decided to hold on to their hurt and anger.

In the short term, it looks like trust will fail. But in the long run, trusting offers a much better life than living in an angry, paranoid state of distrust. You may think that keeping the anger will protect you from future hurt. Not so. By putting up your anger shield, you will be more likely to be betrayed or deceived.

I learned this principle as a college student while being trained to sell encyclopedias door to door by a master salesman. I saw a sign on the front door that said *No Peddlers or Solicitors.* I said to my trainer, "We cannot go there."

He said, "Yes, we can. They are the most vulnerable ones on the street. That is why they put up the sign."

We knocked on the door and in a few minutes, we were in the house selling the books.

One of the personality tests I use in pre-hiring assessments has a trust–mistrust scale. The research behind it reveals how those who highly mistrust people are very vulnerable to being deceived.

Howard E. Butt, Jr., in his book *Who Can You Trust? Overcoming Betrayal and Fear,* writes about "Our Trust vs Mistrust Dilemma." He quotes an old English proverb: *It is an equal failing to trust everybody, and to trust nobody.*

Our lives, families, democracy, investments, health, travel, and diet are all built on a foundation of trust. If you did not trust, you would not get out of bed in the morning. You might even fear that the bed or house would collapse around you; you might think your food was poisoned so you would die of malnutrition.

Butt says:

Trust holds life together.[8]

Trust verses mistrust battle rages around and within us.[9]

Each trust versus mistrust conflict is so personal, so close.[10]

You and I can attest to the fact that we have trusted and then been very hurt, even when we started out convinced that the person we were trusting was trustworthy. We become confused because a person we had always trusted suddenly betrays us.

You and I get to decide: Will we live a life carefully picking who we will trust, or will we not trust anyone? One of these paths leads to a lonely, isolated, unfulfilled life. Can you guess which one?

Yes, betrayal of a trust is very painful and sometimes we think we will never get over it. The fact is some don't and choose to live a life of constant fear. When fear is excessive and dominates one's life, it is often labeled *paranoid*. But you have the choice to live in the past with its pain or rise up to the challenge of a new day and a new life.

I recall a mother and daughter who lived together and were social friends of mine. I never knew the full story about the deceased husband who had been an alcoholic and abusive to the family. The elderly mother was a wonderful, warm, friendly lady. The daughter was cold and closed off and never married. They lived through the same situation yet chose to respond very differently.

Betrayal leads to mistrust, which leads to chaos, which can lead to despair. "Chaos is the despair and horror you feel when you have been profoundly betrayed."[11]

The reason we feel this way is because all that we trusted and counted on now seems destroyed, *but it is not all destroyed,* it just feels like it is. Trust gives us order and predictability in our lives. Without trust, we have to question and doubt all that we do and everyone we encounter.

It is okay to experience a short period of chaos and despair; that is normal after a painful betrayal. However, we must not choose to make that our life. It is okay to let the birds fly over our heads but not okay to let them build a nest in our hair. We must get up and get going again, in spite of the pain.

There is no such thing as not choosing. At some level you will make a decision. The decision to get up and move on is initially much more difficult than taking the victim road by default, which is all downhill. Do you want to live the life of a victim, complaining, "Woe is me," and being depressed, bitter, and resentful?

The world-renowned Alfred Adler, an Austrian psycho-therapist, would ask his patients, "What are you getting out of this?"

Many times, I have used his question. Some want to resist and say, "Nothing."

If Adler's patients responded this way, he would retort with something like, "So why are you keeping it?"

The fact is, any of our self-beliefs, attitudes, or behaviors has some kind of payoff or we would not keep it. The one who chooses to stay a victim usually gets pity and has an excuse for not living a healthy, productive life. They feel they have the right to remain angry and miserable. They get to wallow in their self-pity.

I wonder what Judas thought he was going to get out of betraying Jesus? While we really do not exactly know, some have postulated that he desired a place of power when Jesus became king or overthrew the Romans. Whatever payoff he thought he was going to get, it did not turn out as he had planned.

Second Primary Hurt

The second primary hurt that comes from betrayal is loss. Loss plays a major part in our lives. We start losing the day we are born, starting with losing the nice, warm, safe place we had in our mother. We spend our lives trying to get and acquire things and friends so that if we lose one, we will not be destitute. It is interesting to observe hoarders on TV. Many hoard because they have had deprivation or fear of deprivation. Some were victims of betrayal, or perhaps a loved one died, or they were physically deprived.

As we said at the beginning of this chapter, loss is very personal. No two people experience it the same way or to the same degree. Some of the dynamics of loss are:

- **What do you have left?** This is a key question. If you lose one friend and that person is your only friend, then you'll experience this loss as more significant than if you had many other friends who could support you.

- **How much have you invested in them?**

- **Was this your mate or child or someone you lived for?**

- **What else have you recently lost?** If you have lost a lot, then you may experience this loss more painfully.

- **How fragile is your self-esteem?** If you already are full of self-doubt, then any loss is likely to hurt you more than it would someone who has solid self-esteem.

- **How important was this person or thing in your life?** You are the only person who can measure this. Perhaps you lost your favorite pet, maybe a dog. This dog could have been your comforter or companion. Someone else may see a dog as a nuisance, nothing to pay attention to.

Obviously, the person who sees dogs as nuisances won't experience the loss of a dog as painfully as you will.

Betrayal Trauma

In 1991, Jennifer Freyd, a professor at the University of Oregon, coined the term betrayal trauma. She said that *betrayal trauma* is similar to posttraumatic stress disorder (PTSD). The primary difference is that PTSD is usually caused by fear, while betrayal trauma is usually caused by anger.

It is not uncommon for both fear and anger to be present. Betrayal trauma often, but not exclusively, occurs in people who were dependent on a caregiver when abuse—physical, emotional, or sexual—occurred. It can also occur in extremely dependent spouses.

We have said before, and we are repeating this because it is of primary importance: Do not expect your betrayer to have the same level of hurt or remorse that you do. Usually they will not. If you expect them to, you will have a very difficult time overcoming the hurt and pain.

Accept the fact that they are probably very insensitive. That is why they treated you the way they did in the first place. When I counsel married couples, it is common for me to see a man who has betrayed his mate have a hard time showing genuine remorse; his partner then becomes angry over this. When this happens, the man will sometimes try to fake remorse, but it does not come off well and the conflict increases.

Sometimes a wife does not believe her mate is remorseful—even when he is—because he does not show or express remorse in a way that matches her expectation. I remember the man who apologized and expressed genuine regret. His wife said, "I forgive you, but I will never trust you." They continued to work on their marriage, and they are still together many years later.

A Myriad of Feelings

When dealing with the pain of betrayal, one can experience a variety of emotions simultaneously. There can be the deep pain of broken trust, and the joy of relief now that you finally understand why your relationship has been so difficult for so long. You may feel anger at what your mate did and fear because now you do not know how you are going to financially care for yourself and the children. You may be embarrassed and concerned about how your friends and family will see you. It's not unusual to have a wide range of feelings that may vary from day to day.

You can find meaning in your despair as well.

It's Not Your Fault

It's not your fault.

It's not your fault.

It's not your fault.

Ten times Sean, the psychiatrist (played by Robin Williams) repeated those words to Will Hunting, the title character in the movie *Good Will Hunting* (played by Matt Damon). Will was an exceptionally brilliant university student who was greatly underperforming and was on a self-destructive path. At the point where Sean was pushing Will to acknowledge that he was not responsible for the cigarette burns and other forms of abuse he endured as a child, it appeared for a moment that Will was going to punch Sean.

Sean knew that unless he could get Will to accept that he was not responsible for the abuse, he could never recover and become the person he was capable of being. Sean knew the first step to recovery was getting his client to accept that he was not responsible.

You and I are like Will. We must understand and accept that the first step to overcoming betrayal is to get rid of our feeling of responsibility for the betrayer's behavior. You may have to say to yourself over and over again—ten times or possibly hundreds—"It's not my fault. It's not my fault. It's not my fault." And you may find it very helpful to watch this movie.

In working with a client, I too have pushed many people to accept that the betrayal is not their fault. It is interesting because one can rationally talk about the betrayer's terrible behavior yet still blame oneself. You must accept and deeply believe that you are not responsible before you can heal and overcome the betrayal. It can be a colossal internal battle to come to full acceptance.

There is a great difference between someone quietly saying it is not their fault, like Will does when Sean starts his litany, and coming to grips with it deep in their psyche and soul, like Will does by the time Sean is done. For some reason, we may want to feel like a victim; we want to feel guilty. Somehow we often feel the guilt makes us feel noble.

Brennan Manning, in his book *The Rabbi's Heartbeat*, says, "What is denied cannot be healed."[12]

I recently read a book review by a psychologist who believed that the victim was often partially responsible for the betrayal. He wrote that there is the possibility we "co-created the climate of betrayal." I completely reject this type of blame. If you (the betrayer) don't love or like your mate or friend, then be a man or woman and step up and face them. Don't be a coward and hide behind betrayal. Cowards betray; people of courage stand up and are honest about what they think and feel.

Three Ways to Overcome the Pain of Betrayal

There are a limited number of effective ways to overcome emotional pain. Sorry—there are no magic potions. Overcoming betrayal is hard work, but these methods are time-tested and well-proven.

Admit the Truth

Admit that you have been betrayed or deceived. Don't pretend that the betrayal did not hurt or affect you. It does hurt and sometimes terribly too, so much so that it feels like it is tearing your guts out or your heart is broken into many pieces.

If you don't admit the truth—especially to yourself—then you are only deceiving yourself. That act of self-deception and betrayal may cause greater harm than the betrayal that was done to you. Having someone lie to you—even when the you is you—is a form of betrayal, a form of breaking trust.

Author Susan Forward, in her book *When Your Lover is a Liar: Healing the Wounds of Deception and Betrayal*, is writing to women in the quote below, but what she writes applies to men as well.

> When your lover is a liar, you and he have a lot in common—you're both lying to you…. He uses denial to keep the truth from you. You use denial to keep the truth from yourself as well. When his lies are discovered, he rationalizes to justify his lying. And so do you.[13]

Lying to oneself is a destructive device we use to try to protect ourselves from facing the truth and dealing with the pain and moving on.

Talk

The magic of counseling is talking. Talking to a professional allows you to hear what you are saying. Something powerful happens once the words come out of your mouth and you hear your own story with your own ears. We gain much more clarity and get to the "aha" moment.

Talking to a very good listening friend can be helpful as well, especially one who is trustworthy, won't judge you, and won't tell you what to do.

Forgive

You must decide to forgive if you want to be free of the pain and move on in life. Many people hesitate to do this because they make some wrong assumptions about the process.

Forgiveness does *not* mean:

- You must open yourself up to be hurt again. That is not necessary in forgiveness. You may choose to, if you believe the relationship is worth saving. But if you do, you must do so slowly and carefully.

- It does not mean that you will automatically forget what happened. The brain just does not work that way. The old expression "forgive and forget" is not so easy. You may need to remember in order to protect yourself from repeating a situation in which you set yourself up to be betrayed again. But remembering is not the same as being suspicious of everyone. Our brain is created in such a way that we are designed to remember. Remembering may keep us from repeating the same mistakes. Remembering allows us to remember the good things in life like our friends and children and happy days. Remembering is not selective where I can choose to completely forget the bad stuff and only remember the good.

You may not feel like forgiving. You may instead feel like getting even. The decision to forgive is difficult, one that almost goes against your grain. It requires you to follow your mind, not your feelings. And do what is good for you. Not something that will make you feel better just for the moment.

At a recent seminar I heard clinical psychologist Janis Abrahms Spring refer to her book *How Can I Forgive You? The Courage to Forgive, The Freedom Not To.* She said, "Not forgiving makes you feel powerful and in control, but it's a reactive, often rigid and compulsive response to violation that cuts you off from life and leaves you stewing in your own hostile juices."[14]

Spring discourages therapists from allowing the betrayed client to make a quick decision to forgive because it rarely brings the client face to face with what really happened and instead buries the hurt deeper in the client. "Cheap forgiveness is a quick and easy pardon with no processing of emotion and no coming to terms with the injury. It's a compulsive, unconditional, unilateral attempt at peacemaking for which you ask nothing in return."[15] She goes on to say that cheap forgiveness offers an out for people who avoid conflict.

When you say no to forgiving, what started as a self-protective solution to pain—a way of coping with your indignation—ultimately leaves you cold and bitter. What held out the promise of restoring your self-regard, creating emotional and physical safety and providing a just resolution to the injury, doesn't deliver—or delivers at a dear price.[16]

Benjamin Franklin said, "Doing an injury puts you below your enemy; revenging one makes you but even with him; forgiving it sets you above him."

Just when you think you have forgiven someone for their wrongdoing, something will come up that will stir up the old experience and hurt feelings. This is when you must actively remind yourself that you made a decision to forgive and you *must* do it again. You will have to forgive many times.

Over time and each time, it will get easier and easier, until finally the old feelings will no longer be dredged up and you will go happily on your way—free.

Again, this is purely mind over feelings. Will you let your feelings rule you? Or will you choose to be the master of your life?

I had the privilege of hearing Kim Phuc Phan Thi tell her story of forgiveness. Kim, who is now an adult, was caught in a napalm bombing when she was a little girl living in South Vietnam. A photographer captured her image as she ran down the road naked and burning; the photo came to epitomize the Vietnam War. (The photographer quickly took her to a hospital.)

Kim has an amazing story and tells that even as she was healing, she knew she needed to forgive those responsible, even though her village's religion did not even have a word for *forgiveness*. She went to a library and started searching for information on the word. The only book she found the answer in was a Bible, which she had never seen before. I encourage you to read her autobiography, *Fire Road: The Napalm Girl's*

Journey through the Horrors of War to Faith, Forgiveness, and Peace. It may help you see that if she could forgive—even though she initially did not know how to—you can too. You probably know how and have done it many times but for some reason this time is harder.

Prayer

In addition to the three methods of overcoming betrayal mentioned above (and recognized by most therapists), I add a fourth: prayer.

If you are a religious person you may already be praying. If you are not religious, you may have found yourself praying. In either case, prayer is good for the soul. It cleanses the mind and soul. It is not about praying for revenge or ruminating on the old hurt. It is about asking for peace and the will to forgive and move on with your life. You will have reached the apex of forgiveness when you can pray for your abuser.

Points to Ponder

1. How am I at forgiving?

2. Have I forgiven the first, last, and all the other times people have hurt me?

3. If I am holding onto hate and revenge, is that making my life better and more peaceful? If not, as the old adage goes, "How is that working out for you?"

Chapter 13

Growing Beyond Betrayal

Once you have admitted your hurt and have taken the step to start forgiving, you are now ready to move on with your life. If, on the other hand, you have not worked on overcoming in a healthy way, you will most likely remain stuck in your personal and emotional development. In fact, you will not just stay stuck where you are; you will actually start to go downhill because there is no such thing as remaining static or maintaining a perfect balancing point.

Think of a teeter-totter. At best, you and your partner could stay balanced for only a few seconds at a time. Growing beyond betrayal is similar. You can stay at a spot of balance for just a little while. You will either move forward and grow, or you will move backward and regress. As Howard Butt says in his book *Who Can You Trust?*, "This dark side of betrayal is allowing ourselves the satisfaction of a harbored bitterness …. Will we turn our feelings away from hatred and toward forgiveness, or will we continue to hold revenge in our hearts?"[1]

When I lived in Toronto, I would frequently visit Niagara Falls and enjoy watching the mighty power of the water crash over the twenty-story precipice. If you are canoeing down the Niagara River, you will reach a point of no return above the Falls where you'll be captured by the current and you'll be doomed well before you go over the Falls. The same is true for you if you keep your resentments. You may think you are happily canoeing along with your resentments; however, you will reach a point of no return where your heart is so hard that it is impossible to navigate to a safe shore. Before you get to that critical point, decide now to paddle your resentment canoe to the shore and head for safety.

As human beings, we are the only beings in all of creation who have the ability to make a conscious decision to not avenge. Yes, deciding to move forward without exacting revenge may make us vulnerable to being hurt again. But that is true whether you forgive and move on, or whether you stay in revenge–bitterness mode. Revenge and bitterness do not insulate you from hurt; they only make you more vulnerable. There are many posters available with the famous quote, "The tragedy of life is what dies inside a man while he lives."

In my book *The Hole in Your Heart,* I have a chapter titled, "The Walking Dead—Are You One of Them?" I wrote:

> The question is not whether some individuals have emotional pain and others do not. We have already established that we all have some degree of pain. The question then is how much pain does each of us carry and how do we choose to cope with it?[2]

Alfred Adler, the Austrian psychologist, says, "No experience is a cause of success or failure. We do not suffer from the shock of our experiences, the so-called trauma, but we make out of them just what suits our purposes."[3]

We get to choose if we want to live in chaos or order. Chaos is when you have unresolved life issues. Order is when you master your mind and emotions. Living an orderly, stable life is much more pleasant than living in confusion, fear, and unresolved anger.

Backus and Chapain, in their book *Telling Yourself the Truth,* raise the key question in Chapter 2, "Do We Really Want to Be Happy?"[4] That is a critical question you need to ask yourself. No one can answer the question for you. Each of us must, and we must answer it every day. No one can make you happy or unhappy.

Some of you, I fear, have chosen to hold on to the betrayal and wear it as a badge of honor, hoping it will give you attention and pity. It may give you both, but it will not give you happiness and contentment.

We can stay stuck in our present unhappiness, fooling ourselves that we are happy. Deceiving yourself is the worst kind of deception and betrayal.

Yes, you have been deceived and betrayed by someone. Are you now going to live a life deceiving yourself that all is well? That is like walking through a hall of distorted mirrors at a circus, mirrors that no longer show you what you really look like but instead make you look extremely tall or short or heavy or thin. There you can laugh at yourself; however, deceiving yourself is not a laughing matter. It is a matter of life and death. So, let's resolve the past and happily move on.

The Need for Meaning

One way to move on is to find meaning in what happened to you and look beyond it to find meaning in life.

Viktor Frankl, in addition to writing his book *Man's Search for Meaning*, is also known for his theory of psychotherapy called logotherapy.

Logotherapy focuses rather on the future, that is to say, on the meanings to be fulfilled by the patient in his future.[5]

According to logotherapy, this striving to find a meaning in one's life is the primary motivational force in man.[6]

Scott Peck opens his bestseller *The Road Less Traveled* with the line, "Life is difficult."[7] Yes, it is; almost no one would disagree. You are going to experience emotional and physical hurt, rejection, betrayal, and loss. You are going to become tired, disappointed, discouraged, and maybe even depressed. I hope not, but you may even experience horrible things like abuse, serious accidents, the death of a loved one, financial loss, and possibly even poverty. Unfortunately, this is life.

Tolstoy, considered one of the world's greatest authors, looked at life through a fatalistic lens. He could only identify four means of escaping from destructive, hopeless thoughts. First was to retreat into childlike ignorance of the problem; the second was Epicureanism or pursuing mindless pleasure. The third was to destroy life once one has realized that life is evil and meaningless. The fourth was continuing to drag out a life that is evil and meaningless, knowing that nothing will come of it. Tolstoy was so fatalistic that he lived much of his life fearing that he would take his own life.

There is another way to look at life. You can live a fulfilling and meaningful life. Because you are a human and you have the ability to give your mind precedence over your feelings, you can decide on a meaningful life. Many would agree that a meaningful life is one where you contribute to your fellow man, who is on a similar journey.

The Need for Deep Roots

So why is it that some experience difficult challenges and still thrive and others live a life of despair? Why do some trees stand strong in a great storm while others get uprooted?

It all has to do with the root system. Put down deep healthy roots and your chance for survival is much greater.

I have worked in prisons, a suicide counseling center, and counseling rooms. I have worked with people behind bars and CEOs of Fortune 500 companies. Every person I know has gone through hard times, including me. This is life.

My view and the view of many is that you must get outside yourself in order to thrive and not be part of the walking dead. As long as you stay in your little life and think only of yourself, you will struggle when the storms of life batter.

There is a way to overcome betrayal and battle back to a meaningful and purposeful life. And when the old hurt resurfaces—because it will—there is a way to get through it. You don't have to become a cynic, like Tolstoy, to overcome the challenges of life.

Find Your Purpose

There are four things you must do to find a meaningful, purposeful, thriving life.

1. Get out of yourself

2. Forgive

3. Learn to love

4. Set new positive goals

You may not like the answer, but it works. Living for money, power, or fame will not fulfill your inner quest for meaning. You may repress your need for meaning, but sooner or later unhappiness or boredom will set in.

The question is not, is there a way forward to a more contented, peaceful life? The question is, are you willing to make the decision and take the action necessary? And believe it or not, the action is not that difficult. Stop talking or ruminating. Just start doing.

Get Out of Yourself

Getting out of yourself is the first requirement—and a well-known secret! If you want to establish meaning and purpose in your life, give, help, and serve others.

Daily look for opportunities to help. You don't even need to look for opportunities; just respond when the opportunity is there to give another person a little lift. It may be just a smile, or a word of encouragement. And most likely, you will get more out of it than they.

Recently a friend asked me what I thought about "a calling." I think we are all called to help, serve, and assist other human beings. That is what separates us from barbarians. No one who does this is weaker for it or unhappy.

I am not suggesting you be a rescuer. Be a helper. There is a big difference. A rescuer often becomes the persecutor when trying to "rescue" and they put a big burden on the other.

As I got through my own experiences of betrayal, others who had been betrayed or rejected seemed to find their way to me, seeking my help. Somehow, the hurting can "sniff out" those who have had similar experiences and dealt with them successfully.

One way you'll know you are doing well in facing your own hurt is that you are ready to help others deal with their rejection or betrayal in a healthy way.

Henri Nouwen was a Dutch Catholic priest and scholar who had taught at several major universities, including Harvard, and still felt very unfulfilled. It was not until he met Jean Vanier in Canada and worked for a short time with the L'Arche community—individuals with severe intellectual disabilities—that he found purpose and meaning. Nouwen quickly found that the people he was working with were giving him more than he was giving to them. He decided to spend the remainder of his life among these genuine people.

In his book *The Wounded Healer*, Nouwen develops the theme that if we have been wounded and come through healed, we are then qualified to be healers. He goes on to say, "Compassion must become the core and even the very nature of authority .... Compassion is born when we discover in the center of our own existence not only that God is God and man is man, but also that our neighbor is really our fellow man."8

Remember how the world admires and respects Mother Teresa for her work among the extreme poor in the slums of Calcutta? I have never heard anyone say they thought she was stupid for what she did. Anyone who knows anything of her story admires her. Isn't it interesting how we admire her, but we are unwilling to do the same? We don't want to serve those in our local neighborhoods, much less Calcutta.

Do you know who you are and what you are meant to do on this earth? You probably have an idea. The question is, will you do it?

Forgive

Forgiveness is the second way to grow beyond betrayal. Yes, we referred to forgiveness in the last chapter about overcoming the pain of betrayal. Here, we are talking about making it a continuous part of your life because it is core to every healthy life.

Some of you may be thinking that forgiveness is a religious thing, so it does not apply to you because you do not consider yourself to be religious. Yes, it is a religious thing for those who are religious, but it is also a primary component of a mentally healthy life. Every therapist, psychologist, and psychiatrist recognizes forgiveness to be absolutely essential to a healthy, free life.

Forgiveness is really not that difficult. All we have to do is get over our pride and anger. You have forgiven others many times. But in this case, this betrayal seems to have hurt you so deeply that you say you "can't forgive." May I suggest that it's not that you *can't*; it's that you *won't*. You have forgiven before and you can do it again. And again. And again.

As the old saying goes, "To forgive is to set a prisoner free and discover the prisoner is you."

The question is not, can you, but *will you*—forgive?

Learn to Love

Love is the third requirement of growing beyond betrayal. Like forgiveness, love is something you know how to do and have done many times. The problem is not that one doesn't know how to love, but that one is so selfish with it. We want to hoard it. It is like bread; if one hoards bread, the bread will soon go moldy and be useless.

Love does not diminish when you give it away. It multiplies. Genuine love is to be concerned for others and do what you can to assist them on their journey. *In Man's Search for Meaning,* Viktor Frankl has written, "Love is the ultimate and the highest goal to which man can aspire…. *The salvation of man is through and in love.*"[9]

Martin Luther King, Jr., said:

And I say to you, I have also decided to stick with love, for I know that love is ultimately the only answer to mankind's problems. [*Yes*] And I'm going to talk about it everywhere I go. I know it isn't popular to talk about it in some circles today. [*No*] And I'm not talking about emotional bosh when I talk about love; I'm talking about a strong, demanding love. [*Yes*] For I have seen too much hate. …I say to myself that hate is too great a burden to bear.[10]

Jason Redman, a Navy Seal who was seriously wounded in Afghanistan and endured thirty-seven surgeries, posted this on his hospital room door:

Attention to all who enter here. If you are coming into this room with sorrow or to feel sorry for my wounds, go elsewhere. The wounds I received I got in a job I love, doing it for people I love, supporting the freedom of the country I love. I am incredibly tough and will make a full recovery.

What is full? That is the absolute utmost physically my body has the ability to recover. Then I will push that about 20 percent further through sheer mental tenacity. This room you are about to enter is a room of fun, optimism, and intense rapid regrowth. If you are not prepared for that, go elsewhere.[11]

Are you ready to live your life to the freest and fullest, focusing on how you can be an encouragement to your fellow man?

Set new positive goals

Life is all about goals. Whether we consciously or unconsciously hold to them. It is universally accepted in the mental health world that we will automatically move in the direction of our goals. People who hold hatred or bitterness or a plan to someday get even will eventually do something they are shocked to find themselves doing and then deeply regret it. Then say, "That was not me." Sorry, well, it was in you and may have lain dormant for a long time.

The same principle is true when you plan to live a life of being kind, helpful and contributing in a positive way. You will find yourself automatically doing good things to others.

It is your choice and I hope and want to encourage you to happily go down the road of love and service regardless of your profession or position in life.

In my case, as a young adolescent, when my father deserted us and gave our family the Judas Kiss, I was very angry. I became far from a nice guy. After about ten years of deep anger, I knew I had to face him to try and get the rage out of my system. I recognized that my anger was seriously affecting me and many relationships. I decided I did not want to spend my life being angry at him. And becoming like him.

I previously referred to meeting my father about ten years after he left us. Now I want to expand on that and make a significant closing comment. My visit was the first time I'd seen or had any communication with him since he left. Without any prior notice, I knocked on his door. When he answered, he said, "Who are you and what do you want?" Of course, he did not know me. I introduced myself and, after he took a moment to gather himself, he invited me in.

I stayed a few days. I saw that he was a pathetic, narcissistic alcoholic. I realized how fortunate I was that he had left us, because my life would have been worse had he stayed.

As I walked across the yard from his home to my car, I looked up to the heavens and said, "God, I am glad he left because if he had stayed in our home, my life would have been much worse." And his impact on my development would have been even more destructive than it was.

As this realization came to me, all my anger and bitterness instantly evaporated.

Two Closing Thoughts for You

I have two closing thoughts to share with you.

First, my message to you is to take a serious look at how bad things may have become if your betrayer had continued to infect your life for many more years. Be thankful that your betrayer finally showed their true colors and that now you can move on in your life instead of being stuck in the land of anger, uncertainty, anxiety, or self-doubt. Celebrate that you are now free. Set some new goals and visions that are meaningful. Not goals for money or power or influence. Rather, say, "I will be a happier, kinder, more giving, more loving, more empathetic person."

Remember, it could have been worse.

Second, remember the words that Robin Williams repeatedly said to Matt Damon in *Good Will Hunting,* words that Matt Damon's character did not want to hear: "It is not your fault. It is not your fault. It is not your fault."

Remember, it could have been worse.

And it is not your fault.

All the best on your new journey! Enjoy life! Have fun!

How We Learn to Betray

Life is about learning. There are several different ways we learn. However, the most common is by watching and observing another's behavior.

In graduate school I was introduced to the writings of Dr. Edwin Sutherland (1883–1950), a highly acclaimed sociologist who is still recognized for his theory of differential association. The theory has a complex name, but very practical application. It offers an explanation of deviant behavior and how one becomes a criminal.

Sutherland proposed that people learn the how and why of criminal behavior through interacting with others who are already criminals. While Sutherland's theory of differential association is focused on deviant behavior, it is also recognized as a theory of learning, or how we learn any behavior—positive or negative.

I have studied and tested this theory many times over the years. In working with betrayers, I have observed that most of them were taught directly or indirectly by a significant person or persons in their life. For example, I know of a case where the mother deceived and betrayed her husband. Her son followed exactly in her footsteps to deceive and betray other family members. Of course, she would deny that she taught him this behavior, for to do so would be to admit to her own misdeeds.

When working in the prison, I was especially intrigued by how frequently I would hear one inmate teach another how to perform a criminal act. Of course, the amusing part was that the "teacher" was in prison for being caught doing what he was teaching.

To simplify the theory, just watch a small child emulate his or her parent.

Sutherland's theory comprises nine principles of learning. Again, he is focused on criminality. I have adapted them below to describe how we learn to betray.

1. We learn to betray from other individuals.

2. We learn to betray as we communicate with one another.

3. We learn most of the patterns of betrayal from people we are close to.

4. We learn not only how to commit the betrayal; we also learn our "why" and how to rationalize our betrayal.

5. We learn that the act of betrayal is something that will be to our benefit or to our detriment.

6. We choose to commit the act of betrayal when we determine that the betrayal is "worth it."

7. We don't need to spend a long time with someone who has betrayed in order to learn this behavior.

8. Learning betrayal by association with other betrayers is like learning any other behavior—positive or negative.

9. Betrayal cannot be explained by a person attempting to satisfy their own needs or values; one can satisfy one's own needs and values by not betraying another. In other words, one does not have to betray another to meet one's own needs or values.

Notes

Chapter 1

1. Howard E. Butt, Jr., *Who Can You Trust? Overcoming Betrayal and Fear* (WaterBrook Press, 2004), 154.

2. Alfred Adler, *Understanding Human Nature* (Greenwich, CT: Premier Books, 1954), 133.

3. Ibid.

Chapter 2

1. Everett Shostrom, *Man the Manipulator* (New York: Bantam Books, 1972), 3–4.

2. Ibid., 15.

3. Ibid., 15–17.

4. Everett Shostrom. *Healing Love* (New York: Bantam Books, 1978), 26.

5. Ibid., 10.

Chapter 4

1. Nathan Ackerman, *Treating the Troubled Family* (New York: Basic Books, 1970), 108.

2. The Institute of Family Studies email newsletter (Charlottesville, VA: Institute for Family Studies, January 10, 2020).

3. Ibid.

4. Edward Kruk. *Psychology Today,* April 25, 2013. https://www.psychologytoday.com/us/blog/co-parenting-after-divorce/201304/the-impact-parental-alienation-children. Retrieved September 20, 2020.

5. Janet Woititz, *Struggle for Intimacy* (Deerfield Beach, FL: Health Communications, 1985), 4, 13, 15, 16.

Chapter 6

1. Alexandr I. Solzhenitsyn, *The Gulag Archipelago* (New York: Harper & Row, 1976), 615.
2. Psalm 55:12–14. The New International Version.

Chapter 7

1. Viktor E. Frankl, *Man's Search for Meaning* (New York: Washington Square Press, 1985), xx.

Chapter 8

1. William Glasser, *Take Effective Control of Your Life* (New York: Harper & Row, 1984), 53.
2. William Glasser, *Reality Therapy* (New York: Perennial Library, 1965), xii.
3. Ibid., 63.
4. Ibid., 69.
5. Ibid., xiii.
6. Peggy Papp, *The Process of Change* (New York: The Guilford Press, 1985), 10.
7. Janis Abrahms Spring, *How Can I Forgive You?* (New York: Harper Press, 2004), 8.

Chapter 9

1. Jordan B. Peterson, *12 Rules for Life: An Antidote to Chaos* (Toronto: Random House Canada, 2018), 99.
2. Viktor E. Frankl, *The Unconscious God* (New York: Simon & Schuster, 1975), 55–56.
3. Ibid., 69–70.
4. Peterson, 103.
5. Ibid., 104.

Chapter 11

1. Henri Nouwen, *The Return of the Prodigal Son: A Homecoming* (New York: Image Doubleday, 1994), P. xx-xx.

Chapter 12

1. Viktor E. Frankl, *Man's Search for Meaning* (Boston: Beacon Press, 2006), 77.
2. Ibid., 67
3. Ibid., 65.
4. Ibid., 66.
5. Ibid., 82.
6. Ibid., 76.
7. Dale Carnegie, *How to Stop Worrying and Start Living* (New York: Simon & Schuster, 1984), 139.
8. Howard E. Butt, Jr., *Who Can You Trust? Overcoming Betrayal and Fear* (WaterBrook Press, 2004), 97.
9. Ibid., 155.
10. Ibid.
11. Jordan B. Peterson, *12 Rules for Life: An Antidote to Chaos* (Toronto: Random House Canada, 2018), 35.
12. Brennan Manning, *The Rabbi's Heartbeat* (Colorado Springs: NavPress, 2003), 24.
13. Susan Forward, *When Your Lover Is a Liar: Healing the Wounds of Deception and Betrayal* (New York: HarperCollins Publishers, 1999), 83.
14. Janis Abrahms Spring, *How Can I Forgive You? The Courage to Forgive, The Freedom Not To* (New York: HarperCollins, 2004), 9.
15. Ibid., 46.

Chapter 13

1. Howard E. Butt, Jr., *Who Can You Trust? Overcoming Betrayal and Fear* (WaterBrook Press, 2004), 54–55.
2. John Brownlee, *The Hole in Your Heart* (Maitland, FL: Xulon Press, 2008), 54.
3. Alfred Adler (lecture, Adlerian Institute, Toronto, Canada, 1982).

4. William Backus and Marie Chapian, *Telling Yourself the Truth: Find Your Way Out of Depression, Anxiety, Fear, Anger, and Other Problems by Applying the Principles of Misbelief Therapy* (Minneapolis: Bethany House Publishers, 2000), 23.

5. Viktor E. Frankl, *Man's Search for Meaning.* (Boston: Beacon Press, 2006), 98.

6. Ibid., 99.

7. Scott Peck, *The Road Less Traveled* (New York: Simon & Schuster, 1978), 1.

8. Henri J. M. Nouwen, *The Wounded Healer: Ministry in Contemporary Society* (New York: Doubleday, 1972), 40–41.

9. Ibid., 37.

10. Martin Luther King, Jr., *Where Do We Go from Here? Address Delivered at the Eleventh Annual SCLC Convention.* August 16, 1967. https://kinginstitute.stanford.edu/king-papers/documents/where-do-we-go-here-address-delivered-eleventh-annual-sclc-convention. Retrieved October 3, 2020.

11. Original image of sign available on www.jasonredmon.com.

For further information about *The Judas Kiss*
Or to contact the author
Email: john@thejudaskiss.com
Or: thejudaskiss2021@gmail.com